CHEVALIER ROBERT DE LA SALLE.

The Picturesque Ohio

A Historical Monograph

~ C. M. CLARK ~

HERITAGE BOOKS
2010

HERITAGE BOOKS
AN IMPRINT OF HERITAGE BOOKS, INC.

Books, CDs, and more—Worldwide

For our listing of thousands of titles see our website
at
www.HeritageBooks.com

A Facsimile Reprint
Published 2010 by
HERITAGE BOOKS, INC.
Publishing Division
100 Railroad Ave. #104
Westminster, Maryland 21157

Copyright © 1887 C. M. Clark

Index Copyright © 1998 Heritage Books, Inc.

— Publisher's Notice —
In reprints such as this, it is often not possible to remove blemishes from the original. We feel the contents of this book warrant its reissue despite these blemishes and hope you will agree and read it with pleasure.

International Standard Book Numbers
Paperbound: 978-0-7884-0983-7
Clothbound: 978-0-7884-8329-5

Publishers' Introduction.

FITLY celebrating the Four Hundredth Anniversary of the Discovery of America, it is but natural that each section of the Republic should hasten to record its contribution to the building of the Nation, and claim its share in the Nation's wealth and glory. Not harm, but only good, can come from a friendly emulation among the States; for while the Nation must ever be greater than any one of its component commonwealths, it is still true that the glory of the Nation is but the aggregate glory of all the States. The Nation is what the States have contributed to make it; and because we appreciate our common heritage of obligation and of privilege in the Nation, we have a laudable pride in what our own communities have done to make that heritage splendid.

Of all the commonwealths, great empires in themselves, which have helped to make this Republic the marvel of history, none have more reason for honest pride and self-congratulation than those which lie in the fertile valley watered by the Ohio and its tributaries. Touching at their eastern entrance the western base of the Alleghanies, they caught the first influx of that immigration which, as soon as independence was won and peace declared, burst through the mountain barriers, and poured its restless human tides into the great Mississippi Valley. If favorable physical conditions have anything to do with making States certainly they found such conditions, who halted their weather-stained immigrant wagons on the banks of the Muskingum or

Miami, on the rolling table-lands of Kentucky, or amid the trackless forests of Indiana. Here was soil which for ages had fed great forests, to receive its compensation when the generous boughs scattered their leaves under the touch of autumn frosts, until unlimited productiveness awaited the labor of the husbandman. Here were beautiful streams, which had never reflected the face of civilized man, waiting to give like reward to the genius and thrift of the manufacturer, while the broad, sweeping river and its tributaries afforded certain avenues of communication and transportation.

We call Columbus the discoverer of America, and celebrate his exploit with blare of trumpet and flutter of pennon. But would it not be truer to history to call the Genoese navigator *a Discoverer* rather than *the Discoverer* of America? In other words, has not the real America had many discoverers, rather than one or two?

What, after all, did Columbus discover? An island in the sea, a dissevered fragment, so insignificant that to-day we scarcely give it a thought. He died without a dream of the vast territory which his courage, and persistency, and faith had opened to civilization.

What did Columbus know, or those who came after him for three hundred years, of what America held in store for men? To Columbus his voyage meant simply larger scope for the old systems of oppression; more gold for the coffers of kings; more territory for the ambition of conquerors; more slaves for the service of aristocracy. Or, if we must grant him the possession of a religious impulse (which, in the light of all testimony bearing upon his character, seems exceedingly doubtful), it was at best but a desire to extend the power of the tyrannous Roman

PUBLISHERS' INTRODUCTION. 7

hierarchy. To later discoverers remained the vision of an almost boundless continent, into whose exhaustless stores God had opened wide the door, inviting the oppressed of earth to broadest liberty, to unparalleled prosperity, and to the building of a new civilization, whose corner-stone should be the freedom of the individual conscience. If our neighbors of Roman Catholic faith simply vied with others, as citizens of a common country, heirs of a common heritage, in extolling the liberties and glories of the Republic, all would welcome their enthusiasm. But we can not accept America at the hands of Rome. Only by its providential deliverance from Spanish domination has the vast territory of the United States and Canada escaped the fate of Mexico and the South American States.

With this thought the publishers send forth this volume. We would not minify the greatness of the *Discoverer*, but we would magnify the courage and foresight and self-sacrifice of the DISCOVERERS. If it required faith and courage and unbending strength of purpose in Columbus to go out over the trackless ocean toward unknown perils, it required no less courage and faith and strength of purpose in La Salle and Boone, and other explorers, to tread the dark forests, enduring exposure and fatigue and hunger, and in constant peril from savage beasts and not less savage men. If his discovery is worthy of grateful commemoration, theirs should not be forgotten. And so it seemed to us that we could make no more fitting contribution to this great anniversary than to send this beautiful volume, recording their deeds of courage and devotion, into thousands of Methodist homes.

We can not forget what history records—that for two hundred years Catholic monarchs and popes struggled in vain for a foothold on the Atlantic Coast; and that they who did at last take possession of it, and laid the permanent foundations of the National life were not Romanists, but Protestants, driven by Romanist persecution from their European homes. Granting that the rocky headlands of the coast were first seen by eyes which adored the crucifix, THE NATION was discovered by men every drop of whose blood cried out against Roman superstition and oppression, and who, with prophetic vision, read God's purposes of emancipation in the opening of the New World. As Methodists, we should be untrue to the memory of our fathers did we permit their part in the planting and building of the Nation to be forgotten. The path of the circuit-rider may be traced all over this great central valley of the continent. His deeds of self-sacrificing heroism are woven into the traditions of every community. He swept like a herald of light from settlement to settlement. Where other ecclesiastical systems, with their formal methods of pastoral supply, were utterly inadequate, the Methodist itinerancy, with such generals as Francis Asbury and Wm. McKendree in command, was fully adequate. The preacher on horseback, with wardrobe and library in the saddle-bags, always ready to move, waiting for no call except the all-inclusive call of God, was just the sort of man for that time. He came with the first settler, and arranged to stay. He came with a genius for organization. His mission was not simply the evangelizing of dissevered communities. He helped to weld the scattered fragments into unity, and so to make possible the Nation. He stimulated the intellectual life of the people. He did not preach a faith which appealed to the ignorance and credulity of its adherents. He advocated the emancipation of the human intellect and will from every thrall of ignorance and superstition. Out of his saddle-bags came the first books that found their way into the remote cabins where citizenship was being formed. He was patron of school and press. It is significant that the very Conference, in 1784, which gave the Methodist Episcopal Church its formal organization, projected a college and pledged its support to higher education, and that among the first enterprises of the new ecclesiastical body was the founding of a house for the publication and dissemination of books. Out of Methodist academies and colleges and universities, scattered all over the valley of the Ohio, have come men and women, cultured in brain and heart, to adorn every walk of life and fill every position of trust, even to the highest in the Republic. Thus, from first to last, along the constantly lengthening lines of National life and power, has Methodism wrought for GOD and COUNTRY.

The publishing-house from which this book issues, is itself at once a product and an exponent of the intellectual life of Methodism in the valley of the Ohio. Started in 1820, simply as a depository for the distribution of Methodist publications, it has steadily increased its facilities to keep pace with growing demands, until its business engages a capital of over a million dollars, and during the past quadrennium there have dropped from its busy presses more than a billion and a half of printed pages.

That this volume may stimulate Christian patriotism in every home to which it finds admittance, and in some measure help to bring this land of ours into the heritage which God reserves for it, and into which HIS TRUTH alone can lead it, is our prayer.

CRANSTON & CURTS, Publishing Agents.

CINCINNATI, *November*, 1892.

CONTENTS.

Part First

HISTORICAL.

CHAPTER I.
"Where the River is Born,"................. PAGE 21

CHAPTER II.
The Discoverer and the Discovery of the River,...... 33

CHAPTER III.
French and English Contests for the Ohio,.......... 53

CHAPTER IV.
Early Settlements,........................ 63

CHAPTER V.
Indian Conflicts on, and for the River, ... 103

CONTENTS.

Part Second.

DESCRIPTIVE.

	PAGE.
AFLOAT ON THE DEEP, SHINING RIVER, ...	187

Appendix.

NOTES, ...	231

ILLUSTRATIONS.

Part First.

	ARTISTS.	PAGE.
Frontispiece: CHEVALIER ROBERT DE LA SALLE,	Crayon by S. J. Ferris, "IVES PROCESS."	
A SUDDEN DARKNESS,	Wm. Hamilton Gibson, Eng. by HARLEY.	17
"WHERE THE RIVER IS BORN,"	A. Cross, Eng. by HARLEY.	21
"LAZILY DROP FROM POOL TO POOL,"	Rhoda Holmes Nichols, Eng. by HARLEY.	23
"CHESTNUT BURRS,"	A. Cross, Eng. by HARLEY.	26
"THE RED LIGHT THE PROUD CARDINAL CARRIES,	A. Cross, Eng. by HARLEY.	27
"A DRAGON-FLY IN SWIFT FLIGHT,"	E. T. Rockwell, Eng. by HARLEY.	28
"A MELANCHOLY JAY-BIRD TELLS THE MOVING STORY OF HER WOES,"	Fidilia Bridges, Eng. by HARLEY.	29
"TO BE PULLED ASIDE AT THE REPRODUCTION OF THE MIRACLE PLAY OF SPRING,"	H. F. FARNY, Eng. by HARLEY.	30
A BEND IN THE RIVER,	Miss Louise McLaughlin, ELECTRO TINT ENG. CO.	32
EARLY DAYS ON "THE SHINING RIVER,"	C. Harry Eaton, "MOSSTYPE" ENG. CO.	52
THREE HUNDRED FEET UP BLACKWATER,	Photo, "MOSSTYPE" ENG. CO.	61

ILLUSTRATIONS.

	ARTISTS.	PAGE.
"A Mountain Tarn,"	Photo, "Ives Process."	91
Indians Fishing in the Allegheny,	H. F. Farny, "Ives Process."	103
Spanning North Fork,	Photo, "Mosstype" Eng. Co.	145
The Cherubs' Roost,	Photo, "Mosstype" Eng. Co.	161
"The Dun Deer that yet linger in the Mountains,"	H. F. Farny, "Ives Process."	182

Part Second.

	ARTISTS.	PAGE.
Up Cheat River,	Bryson Burroughs, "Ives Process."	183
Fishing on the Kanawha,	H. F. Farny,	189
Looking up Elk Creek (Charleston, W. Va.),	Photo, "Ives Process."	195
Bridge over the Ravine,	Vogt, Eng. by WEISBRODT.	210
Plan of Cairo,	Eng. for NATIONAL BANK.	225
View on the Greenbrier,	Burroughs,	230

PART FIRST.

THE
HISTORICAL MONOGRAPH
OF
The Beautiful River.

"A SUDDEN DARKNESS SHROUDS THE CRESTED PEAKS"—Page 23

Chapter I.

Where the River is Born.

THE Ohio River—mountain-born and valley-fed—gathers the

little tributaries of its two formative and its southern affluents from the heights, uplands, ravines and valleys of the western watershed of that section of the Appalachian chain which links the broken spurs of the irregular Catskill to the frowning and rugged ridges of the southern Alleghany.

The sources of these small streams are as varied as are the mountain silhouettes, or the ever-changeful skies above them. They are collected drop by drop in the rain-caverns of the highest peaks, in the slight depressions of the uplifted dells, in the rock-ribbed ravines that flank the crested summits, and from the crystal springs that issue through the ledges of the craggy cliffs. Upon the very topmost heights an occasional silvery line runs over the face of the battlemented steeps; or a miniature flood leaps sheer into space, breaking in silvery drops as it falls into the dusky tarn beneath.

The little wandering rivulets wind about in solitary threads of sinuous trace, until some obstacle of rock or tree brings their reverted coils together; then, as the volume of water increases, the brook hurries over slope and precipice to its outlet from the heights.

Lower down the mountain-side, where the swelling ridges widen, the gathering of the waters begins. The brawling brooks fall together, singing of the cliffs they have left and the dangers they have passed. And now the chorus grows loud and full, for the arching forest aisles echo and re-echo the sound, as the foaming, glittering waves rush over the rocks down to where noise and glitter are lost in the stream that tranquilly glides through long, narrow stretches of emerald-tinted meadows.

But the incoming of the watery tribute is not yet ended; for

through the outlying fields and orchards which cover the slopes that fall from the thickly-wooded hills, and over the shelving descent of the broken uplands, the slow-going little creeks lazily drop from pool to pool as the wrinkling circles send their pulsing currents onward to the "meeting of the waters."

When the broad-bosomed valleys of the rich lowlands are reached, the Ohio gathers its tributaries and goes on to join the Mississippi in its triumphant march to the Gulf.

From their sources upon the giddy heights to where they are lost in their union with the valley streams, each one of the mountain rivulets which contributes to the Ohio perfectly fits into the wild and broken landscape it traverses. The characteristics of rivulet and sylvan landscape are distinctly defined; yet, as counterparts, they thoroughly harmonize.

From where they issue beneath cleft and jutting spur of the cloud-touched ridges, beside tufts of hanging harebells that dot the bold escarpments, to where they come dancing over the edges of the mossy cliffs that brokenly terrace the wide stretches between the forest-crowned peaks, these rippling streamlets are piece and parcel of the wild scenery they serve to illustrate and relieve. They gurgle over rocky beds through dense forests which the morning sun never sees and which the westering sun hardly pierces with its long, shadowy, glimmering rays. In fertile, uplying glades they turn and return until their twisted curves encircle fairy-like bits of woodland scenery to which the noonday splendor of the high levels lends the glamour of enchantment. They wind beneath long vistas of overarching trees, where the gnarled roots are covered with a carpet of tinted mosses in which tiny blue and purple flowers lie hidden. They linger where the waving plumes of flags and of the broad-bladed grasses border the water-line; and where the crimson-spotted trout skim along the shallows, or leap in flame-tinted flashes out of the depths of the still, shadowy pools. Their wavelets creep up the shelving banks to touch the starry-eyed flowers that look out from the gold-broidered stretches of the narrow upland meadows, and they loiter, in changing circles, under the drooping branches of the sweet-scented mountain honeysuckle. If the year is young, and a pattering shower dimples the brook and hurries it over the broken rifts downward, it rushes in mad haste between the jagged boughs of the storm-twisted and flame-scarred trees of the rugged hillside; whirling in noisy flight around the rough clearings, where the leafless skeletons of the wooded belt tell how fire was used to eke out the sharp strokes of the woodman's axe, down to where a sudden turn leads into some secluded valley, suggestive of the fox, the bear, and the dun deer that yet linger in the mountains, and of the stately sachem who once stalked these coverts.

When the icy fetters of winter are fairly broken, when mountain-side and fell are brightened with the white-blossoming dogwood and the rose-hued thickets of the gay red-bud, when the slow-melting floods have reached the lower levels—then the swamp-willows take their first faint tinge of color; the trailing arbutus puts on its pale-rose tint, and all the little sweet-scented things that sleep under the snow are blooming in the wood. The languor and perfume of spring is in the air, the May-apple blossoms hang under their tented leaves, and

"Crowned daffodils are dight in green."

When Spring has taken flight—with her train of delicate beauties—summer comes to the mountains, bringing warmth and richness of color into the wild life that the languorous spring only stirred into a half-awakened existence.

In the hot months Nature scatters her gifts broadcast. Then

the heights are aglow with splendour. The firs are decked with an edging of prickly lace, the pines put on all their bravery of shining

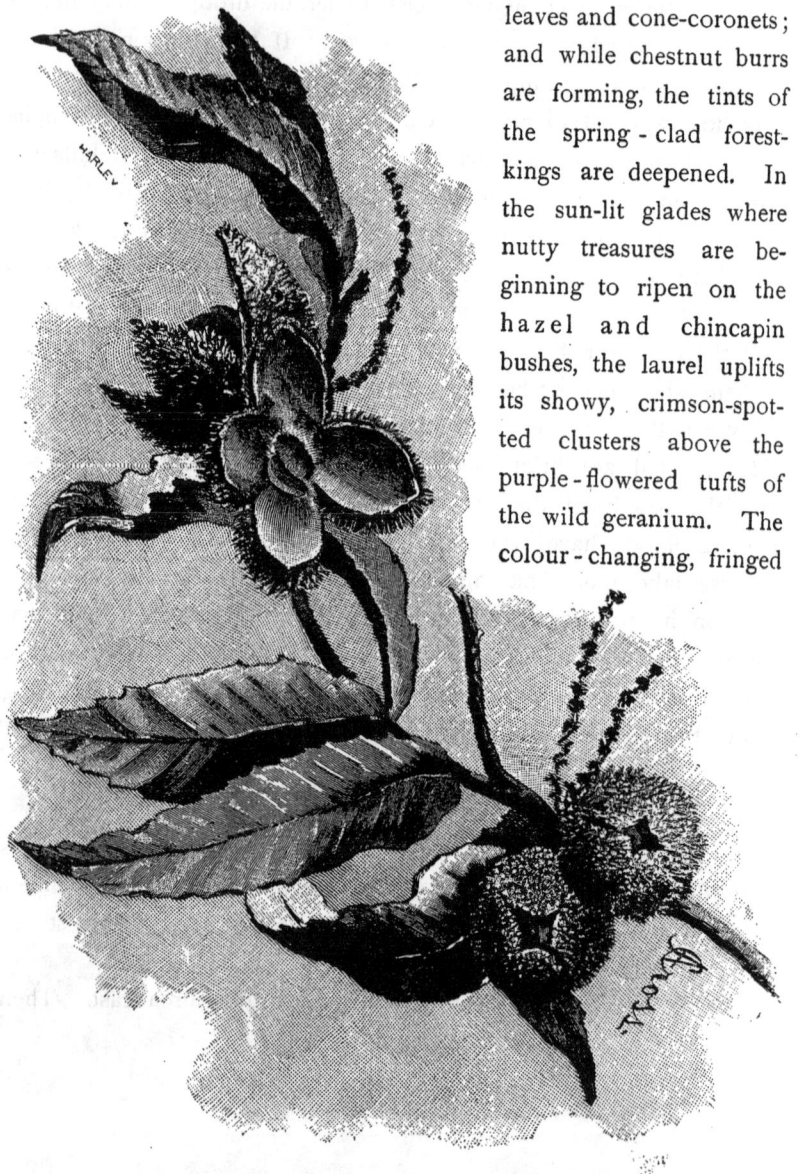

leaves and cone-coronets; and while chestnut burrs are forming, the tints of the spring-clad forest-kings are deepened. In the sun-lit glades where nutty treasures are beginning to ripen on the hazel and chincapin bushes, the laurel uplifts its showy, crimson-spotted clusters above the purple-flowered tufts of the wild geranium. The colour-changing, fringed orchis dots the bank above the brook;—while down below, the trout lazily rise to the thirsty fly that buzzes between sips to his shadow.

In the shelving mountain-passes through which summer streamlets are slowly flowing, the flowers are all on show, — even to those little gadabouts, the ground-ivy and the lace-vine (so named by the mountain folk) befurbelowed in gossamer. The walking-fern has crossed a tiny rill to see the red lights the proud cardinal carries on the top of its tall stalks: while from

every coigne of vantage, of sunny bank or deep, shade-environed dell, the prickly branches

of the wild eglantine uplift, in stately pride, their wealth of opening buds and blossoming flowers. A drag- on-fly in swift flight — called by a question of great pith and mo- ment to an outlying glade on the moun- tain's eastern slope— rests a second on the wing, and then alights on the face of a blushing rose to watch the blue larkspur, which is waving its grace- ful stem from neighbour to neigh- bour, as the merry gossips tell what the thrush whistled to the yel- low-hammer when the mocking- birds fell in- to such a rollicking twitter of laughter.

Hard by the bank, in a gnarled old tree around which a vine has woven a summer screen, a melancholy jay-bird tells the moving story of her woes to a sympathetic but hungry robin which has its near eye flooded with misty drops of pity and its off eye fixed on a fat worm it means to dine upon, when Mrs. Jay ends her story of the heartless woodpecker that kept up its horrible hammering on her house-tree until, between the frights and the falls of the nestlings in trying to see the monster, she lost the last of her promising brood. Before the story is ended, or the worm is caught, a sudden darkness shrouds the crested peaks.

A fierce wind comes shrieking up the pass scattering the watery fragments of the storm-cloud it carries, as it rushes on leaving ruin in its track.

The robin vanishes with the quick-coming storm. The jay's nest falls as the nestlings had fallen; and the melancholy little grass-widow is left to smooth her wet and ruffled feathers—all alone, in a homeless world.

The larkspur and her merry neighbours are lying prone upon the ground, near a broken dragon-fly that is buried beneath the torn petals of a rose. The cardinal-flower has lost its red lights; and the tiny rill—changed to a rain-laden rivulet—sweeps over the track of the walking-fern. The "lace-vine's gossamer furbelows" are torn into shreds, and the flower-covered bank is floating upon a muddy and swollen stream.

But a cloudless night and the sun-kisses of a summer morning, will uplift the fallen and heal the wounded. Where the dead have gone down, there will be an increase of life; but between loss and increase the fructifying winter must come:—a drop-curtain to be pulled aside at the reproduction of the miracle-play of Spring.

A BEND IN THE RIVER.

CHAPTER II.

THE DISCOVERER AND THE DISCOVERY OF THE RIVER.

THE Discoverer of the OHIO, ROBERT RENÉ CAVELIER, was born November 22, 1643, at his father's country-seat, called La Salle, hard by the famous old city of Rouen, in Normandy.

The Caveliers belonged to the *Grande Bourgeoisie*, that untitled class from which the nobility of France was recruited after the autocratic power of the great nobles was curbed by their enforced vassalage to the crown. The father and uncle of young Cavelier were wealthy merchants, and some of the connection held places of trust and honor at Court. That his parents were people of good position in Rouen is evident from the education and breeding of the younger son, who at an early age was placed with the Jesuits, where his ability was recognized and fostered.

It is asserted by several of his contemporaries that before his father's death Robert was designed for the priesthood, and that he had already entered his novitiate. It is probable that this is true, for the existing records prove that he had in some way lost all legal right to a share in his father's estate, and, under the French law of that period, connection with the Jesuits would have entailed its forfeiture.

The scant gleanings that can be gathered from the few letters preserved in the French archives as to the manner of La Salle's early life give the bare facts, that when he was twenty-one years of age he parted with the Jesuits on friendly terms, they giving him excellent testimonials to his scholarly attainments, his good conduct, and his unblemished character; that an annuity of four hundred livres was given him from the inheritance of his father; that an exchange of this annuity for the capital it represented was effected; and that, with this modest sum, he sailed for Canada in 1666 to discover for France the richest possession she has ever let slip from her grasp.

Although history has given but meager data by which to discern so checkered a personality as that of Robert Cavelier, who disappears from the list of Jesuit novices in 1664 to reappear as M. de la Salle in an official report from Patoulet to Colbert, November 11, 1669; though we can not "clothe him in his very habit as he lived," we have sufficient indication of underlying characteristics in the rapid movement of his life, to sketch a man of action whose soul is unveiled in the record of his achievements. That he had a clear intellect and that divining instinct of discovery which, without any traceable process, computes the results that await effort, is demonstrated by his success in the teeth of obstacles that detached from him in his first expedition all following except the devoted, unreasoning Indian, whose higher law was comradeship in danger after the persuasion of prudence had failed. That he was able, ambitious, calm, discreet, enthusiastic, fearless, indefatigable, reticent, self-poised, absolute of will, inflexible of purpose, we learn, through the charges and admissions of his enemies. To these characteristics join the fact that he had in his veins the hot blood of the roving Norsemen, who cut Normandy out of Gaul in the reign of Charles the Simple, and it becomes plain to the most superficial reader of men that La Salle had the qualities and temperament which fitted him for the career he had chosen.

Yet to comprehend the multiform individuality of so complex

a nature, something more than a mere summary of qualities is needed. Any sketch of La Salle, however circumscribed, would be incomplete, if it failed to note the seeming transformation wrought by the changed circumstances of his life.

The metamorphosis of Robert Cavelier into La Salle, of the Jesuit novice into the man of action, who without any previous knowledge of business from his first start in Canada, held his own, and scored success after success in his career as an Indian trader, would be of itself a marvel. But when to this is added the revelation of another and totally different personage, as soon as La Salle feels his foothold secure, when the man of business is merged into the enthusiastic discoverer, in the ambitious aspirant for immortality; and when, through a magnificent recklessness of expenditure, it is made plain that gains were valued only as a means to secure an end; then it becomes necessary to turn back the leaves and make a study of the surroundings, the temperament, and the teaching of Robert Cavelier, that we may understand La Salle. That his connections were people of large wealth, for that age, we know. That his immediate family were devout Catholics is proved by the entrance of two sons into the priesthood. Jean Cavelier, the older son, a priest of the Order of St. Sulpice, was sent to Canada by the superior of the Sulpitians before his brother left the Jesuit Seminary. That Robert entered the seminary when very young is probable; the custom of the time, and his proficiency in mathematics and the physical sciences, warrant that belief.

Of his parents we know but little. His father died before he left the Jesuit Seminary; hints that faintly outline a sketch of his mother can be found in occasional incidental mention of her in connection with business transactions, where money was to be paid. That she was a notable manager is a probability that can be confidently counted in the reckoning. The magnates of the *Grande Bourgeoisie* founded their fortunes upon close economies, and in French mercantile houses—then as now—a man's wife was an active partner. The consideration won, and the position held, by each family of this untitled commercial aristocracy, depended largely upon personal character and the manner in which gains were made. To understand this, one needs to remember that the *Grande Bourgeoisie* was altogether a moneyed supplement to a proud, careless, and usually embarrassed nobility. Consequently, to the moneyed class, placed between the nobles and the people, character was every thing: that established as the permanent distinction of a family, and the good will of the priesthood secured, meant security of position and certainty of advancement through marriage alliances. It is therefore easy to divine Madame Cavelier's position as an autocrat in her family, and in the outer world an austere *dévote* securely placed upon the pinnacle of commercial greatness. A hint that assists in this outline sketch can be gleaned from the respectful ceremony observed by the son in the one letter to her, which is yet in existence. It is a farewell letter, yet there is no spontaneity of feeling in it. Every word gives evidence that attentive observance and a certain courteous phrasing of respectful esteem were more acceptable to "Madame and most honored mother," than frank confidence and unstinted expression of affection would have been. From this letter alone it is made plain that the shy, reticent, repressed boy had been "at odds" with life from its very beginning; and that through failure to understand her son, Madame Cavelier's influence had failed to bind him to the order in which he had been placed.

That the order was a prominent factor in forming Robert Cavelier is beyond question. The qualities that were essentially his, were more or less modified by Jesuit moulding; in fact, it is patent that their training changed in no slight degree many chacteristics of the novice, who afterwards became a bitter enemy of the society he had quitted. Fortunately this moulding so shaped and adapted the subject-pupil for the trying future he was to face, that through its very compression he was much better fitted to deal with the wary, astute savages he was to meet, and with the demi-savages who followed him in the path of discovery.

Through the history of his after life, as well as from the reading between the lines in the brief "Family Papers," there are intimations—mere suggestions to inform judgment—that make it comparatively easy to picture the boy whose enthusiasm was fired, though its outward expression was restrained, by the thrilling narratives of the Jesuit Fathers, who from time to time stopped at the seminary on their way to or from Canada.

These missionaries were fanatical lovers of their order; their ambition for its success was utterly devoid of personality; consequently that ambition, as a wide-spread impersonal flame, was all the more intense. The individual was lost in the association; and it is impossible to overestimate the gain to the association through the character and intelligence merged in its ranks.

To understand the special importance of the time to the Jesuits, it must be remembered that no period in its existence— up to that date—had been so fateful to the Society of Jesus. Canada had been the scene of their disastrous defeat, and they were resolved that upon the same ground a final victory should be won. They had eager rivals in the field; other orders had gained a secure foothold. But the Society of Jesus was a *unit*, and the unit could resolve itself into countless soldiers. Many were already detached, and in the field. Allouez and Marquette were, even then, out upon the extreme border of the colony, at the Gateway of the Lakes, beyond which stretched the unknown territory of the New World.

How fascinating these narratives were to a boy in whose heart the restless Norman current throbbed as stories of battle and of conquest were told, needs no strain of the imagination to understand. Fuel was fed to fire by picturesque descriptions of newly discovered countries, and by the marvelous accounts, which had been gathered from the Indians and from escaped or ransomed captives, of the vast regions yet unexplored. The Fathers told of unnumbered hosts to be saved, of fierce tribes to be conquered. The Cross was to be planted above the broken idols of the heathen, and a great empire was to be added to France.

The dangers told, only lent a new charm to the picture. The realm of fancy never opened to any young enthusiast such rare attractions—such a wealth of wonders. What fire there must have been in the shining eyes when he knew that the Spaniards had not exhausted discovery! Pizarro, De Soto, Cortez had left no successors in Spain. Beyond the New France was an unknown continent where a white man's foot had never trod, and through its mysterious forests a great river flowed westward to the Vermilion Sea—a highway to India, to China, to the trade England coveted, and the glory France might win.

Moved by a new impulse, young Cavelier threw fresh ardor into his daily tasks. Plutarch had taught him what price fortune puts upon her favors. He knew that the day of little things preceded the day of victory, and he began to understand that to win in this great venture, to conquer success, he must be master of himself, untrammeled and free. Then was born the resolve that the general of no order, should have power to call him back when the way opened, and his foot touched the threshold of discovery. The teaching of the Jesuits gave him the weapons that won his freedom. The novice was released from his novitiate. The order lost a priest, whose name would have illumined its annals, the world added a new name to the list of discoverers and heroes.

Robert Cavelier shrinks out of sight as the seminary door closes. But that La Salle carried to Canada a bitter remembrance of some unhealed wound of the spirit, is put in evidence by his sudden and entire estrangement from the order to which he had been partially affiliated, although to the day of his death he was a devoted Catholic and an enthusiast for the spread of the faith. Just here is the problem of his life which no record yet found has unveiled. There is twice, or thrice, mention of a purposed marriage. There is evidence of decided opposition, and—nothing more. In the hands of a novelist the construction of fiction might define the truth which is hidden in this veiled chapter in the life of La Salle.

That part of his life which has to do with our narrative, the story of the discovery of the Ohio, will be given in extracts from the records, which have been preserved in France, and recently published there:

"It happened that an Iroquois chief, Nitarikyk, sent a captive Ottawa to Abbé de Queylus, at Montreal, for something he needed. Being questioned about his tribe, which dwelt far to the south-west, the captive gave such a touching picture of his people, and such an interesting description of his country, that the Abbé wrote to M. Dollier, a Sulpitian missionary, who was passing the Winter with Nitarikyk to learn the Algonquin language, that 'as you have the salvation of the savages at heart, God has here given you by means of this captive an excellent opportunity to carry the cross to nations hitherto unknown to the French; and, to judge from this Ottawa, these tribes are as docile as they are intelligent.' M. Dollier accepted the suggestion, and returned to make his preparation for the enterprise, and to receive from the Abbé de Queylus the necessary orders.

"The governor, M. de Courcelles, advised him to take with him M. de la Salle, brother of Père Cavelier, saying 'they could make the journey more safely together; that M. de la Salle had premeditated for a long time an expedition to find a great river, which he believed, from the accounts given him by the savages, had its course towards the west, but that it would take seven or eight months to get there; that the savages had also told M. de la Salle that this river emptied into the Vermilion Sea; that it was called in the language of the Iroquois *Ohio*; and that upon its banks lived a great many Indian nations, unknown to the French, but so numerous that many of these tribes had from fifteen to twenty villages.'

"He added 'that the expectation of collecting beaver-skins, and the hope which he placed above all others, to find the passage to the Vermilion Sea, into which M. de la Salle believed the Ohio emptied, would make him very glad to undertake the voyage, that he might find through this sea of the South a passage to China.'

"M. de Courcelles will do all in his power to assist La Salle, because 'this discovery will be a glorious gain to France; and, besides, *it will cost the government nothing*.' Governed by these fixed ideas, M. de Courcelles sent to La Salle letters patent which gave him permission 'to search the woods, the rivers, and the lakes of Canada, to find the head of this river.' The governor also recommended him to the governors of all the neighboring provinces with whom France was at peace, and he especially requested the governors of Virginia and Florida to permit him to pass through any portion of their domain, and to give him such assistance as he should need."

The better to assist the expedition the governor recommends M. Dollier to "turn your zeal towards the people living upon the Ohio River, and go with La Salle." Yet considering economy even in spreading the faith, he naïvely adds: "M. de la Salle will make the arrangements for the journey; the governor can only aid by giving permission to take with them as guard certain soldiers who, if paid and provided for, are willing to join the expedition as volunteers."

Having completed their purchases at Quebec, where they bought as many canoes as they could possibly man, and having engaged as large an escort as La Salle could provide for, M. Dollier and M. Barthelmy, who had received permission from the bishop to be of the party, reckoned their united forces. La Salle had five canoes and fourteen men, while Dollier and Barthelmy had two canoes and seven men.

They were ready for the start, and about to leave, when suddenly came from the Abbé de Queylus the suggestion that La Salle might abandon the Church party: "All know his humor to be changeable, and the first whim might influence him to leave you, and that, perhaps, when it would be very necessary for you to have some one who understands the people, and the situation of the country through which you must return. It is imprudent to throw yourselves into the midst of unknown dangers; and at least before starting you should have some assurance as to the route you are likely to take."

The following is the Abbé Gallinée's account of the expedition:

"It was for certain considerations that the Abbé de Queylus permitted me to accompany M. Dollier when I asked his permission. First, because I could be useful, on account of my knowledge of mathematics, in drawing maps of the country through which we should travel, so that in an extremity the party could find their way back without a guide; besides, M. Barthelmy, whose place I took, knew thoroughly the Algonquin language, and thus could be more useful as interpreter at Montreal.

"I had three days in which to make my arrangements. I took two men and a canoe, with sufficient merchandise to buy the necessaries to live upon from the tribes we should meet, and I was ready to embark as soon as the others. The haste with which my preparations were made left me no time to write to the bishop or the governor.

"Our little fleet of seven canoes, each one carrying three men, left Montreal July 6, 1669, led by two canoes of Iroquois (Sonnontouans), who had come to Montreal in the Autumn of 1668 on a hunting expedition, and to make a treaty. These people had lived with La Salle for some months,* and had told him such marvels of the Ohio River (which they said they knew perfectly), that he was more than ever inflamed with the desire to see it. They said 'the river had its origin only three days' journey from Sonnontouan, and that after a month's march we would find the villages of Honniasontkeronons and the Chiouanons, and that after having passed those and the great rapid or fall which is in the river, we would reach the Outagame and the country of the Iskousogos, and in that abundant country deer and buffalo were as plenty as the trees of the wood, while the villages were thickly inhabited.'

"La Salle reported these things to M. Dollier, who became more and more anxious to save the poor savages, 'who, perhaps, would have made good use of the Word of God had it been spoken to them.' The zeal of M. Dollier prevented his remarking that La Salle, who said he perfectly understood the Iroquois, and had learned all these things through his knowledge of their language, knew absolutely nothing at all of it, and, in fact, threw himself headlong into the enterprise without knowing where he was going. He had been led to believe he could find at the village of the Sonnontouans captives from the southern tribes, who would serve for guides. I had been studying Algonquin, but it would have been very much better if I had known more of the Iroquois than I knew of Algonquin. The only interpreter I had been able to find was a Holland Dutchman, who knew Iroquois perfectly, but unfortunately knew very little French; but not being able to find any one else, I took him. M. Dollier and I had intended to pass by Kenté, to speak with our own people who were there in the mission, but our guides were going to the village of Sonnontouan, and we dared not quit them for fear we should find no others."

M. Gallinée continues the story, and tells how they ascended the St. Lawrence, and reached Lake Ontario on the 2d of Au-

---
* Note No. A, in Appendix.

gust, and describes the beautiful country along the rivers which empty into this lake; and he also tells the fact, that "it is by this path the Jesuits go to their missions among the Iroquois, for it is upon the Onnantagué that they have made their principal establishments; this and other rivers which empty into Ontario, are the highways that lead to the Iroquois country."

August 8th, they arrived at an island—

"Where a Sonnontouan chief has built him a secluded country house so well hidden that a passer-by, without knowing the spot, could not find it—a very necessary prudence, as here in the midst of the waters he is also in the midst of his enemies. He received us cordially, and made us welcome to a great feast of stewed pumpkin and roast dog. Our guide advised us to stay here until he should go to the village and give notice of our coming. We were not sure of our lives among these people, and we thought it best to take his advice. Peace had been made but a very short time, a peace with which some of the tribe were dissatisfied; and, as their chiefs are not sovereigns, it was only necessary that some young warrior, who was displeased at the peace, and who remembered the relations he had lost in the war just ended, would be glad to do something which would break the treaty made by the older chiefs. Besides this, a still more serious reason for precaution can be given, from an occurrence which took place about two weeks before our departure from Montreal. Three soldiers who were in the garrison there found that some Indians had a stock of valuable furs, and they assassinated the savages to get them. Happily for us, the crime was discovered five or six days before our departure, the guilt of the criminals was fully proven, and they were shot in the presence of many Indians who happened to be at the fort at the time. The Indians professed to be perfectly satisfied with this speedy execution of justice; however, we knew that though the nation was appeased, the relatives might not be willing to forego their law of retaliation."

After some humane reflections, in which the feeling of distrust was evidently intensified by his own position in the Indian village, the Abbé goes on to say:

"I can assure you that a person who finds himself in the midst of all these fears, with the added alternative of death by famine in the depth of the forest, yet who believes he is there by the will of God, and that his sufferings may be the salvation of these poor savages, realizes a certain joy even in all these pains.

"M. Dollier, though sick of a fever that bid fair to carry him off, said: 'I prefer to die in the midst of this forest, if it be the will of God, which I believe it is, than in the midst of my brothers in the seminary.'"

Notwithstanding this beautiful resignation, M. Dollier soon recovered, and the journey was continued until they arrived at the mouth of a little river, which emptied its waters into the lake not far from the village of Sonnontouan. Here they were "visited by a number of Indian chiefs, accompanied by women laden with presents of wild rice and fruit; in return we gave them knives, needles, and other things which they valued."

The Abbé continues:

"After a consultation among ourselves it was decided that I should go to the village with M. de la Salle to see if we could purchase a captive to guide us to the famous river M. de la Salle had started to find. We took with us eight of our Frenchmen, leaving the rest of our force with M. Dollier to guard the canoes. When near the village we found a troop of old men seated on the ground by the wayside, and they had left us a very comfortable seat in front of them. An old chief, who was almost blind, and who could hardly sustain his weight with the assistance of a staff, stood up and made us a very animated harangue, in which he testified to his joy at our arrival, and that we must regard the Sonnantouans as brothers, and that as brothers he insisted upon our coming to his village, where a lodge was ready for us, and where all waited to know our wishes. We thanked him through the interpreter, and said the next day we would tell his people the cause of our journey. After this exchange of courtesies they conducted us to our lodging, and strict orders were given to the women to let us want for nothing. All that evening and the next morning we saw constantly arriving chiefs who were coming to the council, and the next day (August 13th) we received in the lodge from fifty to sixty of the head men of the nation. When the parley was about to begin, for the first time M. de la Salle admitted that it was impossible for him to make himself understood, and it was very evident that my Dutch interpreter did not know enough French to make us understand what the chiefs were saying. In this extremity we found in our party a man who had been for some time with the Jesuits among the Five Nations, and there was nothing left for us to do but to avail ourselves of such knowledge as he had. Fortunately our presents could speak for themselves. Our first gift to the head chief was a very handsome double-barreled pistol, with the declaration that we regarded the Iroquois as brothers, and with this pistol he would have one barrel for the Loups and the other for the Andostoues. After a general distribution of presents, we declared that we were sent on the part of the governor to visit the tribes living upon the Ohio, and that we wished our brothers the Iroquois to give us a captive as a guide. The chiefs answered that it was necessary to think of this proposition, and they would give us a reply on the next day. The following morning they came early, and after distributing among us numerous presents of beaded work, they came to the question of the captive. They said they would give us such a guide, but begged us to wait until their people, who had gone to make a treaty with the Holland Dutch in New York, and who were now on their homeward journey, should arrive at the village. We agreed to wait eight days longer, excusing ourselves for the limited time, as the season was passing in which we ought to make the journey."

After having suffered no little from the savage messes he was forced through politeness to eat during the time of waiting for the return of the chiefs and the gift of the promised captive, the Abbé concluded to stay his stomach and divert his mind by making a trip with La Salle and two of his Indian friends to see an extraordinary fountain in a neighboring village. This fountain was formed from a little rivulet that fell from a high and broken rock in a considerable stream into a round basin. We let the father describe the spring in his own words, also the arrival of the absent chiefs:

"The water is very clear, but it has a horrible odour, something like the mud of Paris when stirred with the foot. If you touch the spring with a flame it lights up as if it were brandy burning, and it is never extinguished until the rain begins to fall. This flame is regarded by the savages as a mark of abundance or sterility, according to its varying appearance. The water has no peculiarly bad taste.

"While we were gone to see the fountain the chiefs returned, and among them were several relations of one of the men who had been killed at Montreal, and as they were drinking a good deal of the Holland gin which they had brought back, and did not seem to weep so much for their relation as they seemed determined to revenge his death, our position was neither safe nor pleasant.

"At that time I saw the most miserable spectacle I have ever beheld in my life. The chiefs had captured on their way back and brought with them a prisoner, a young boy eighteen or twenty years old. At the entrance of the village they made him run the gauntlet, but as nothing more was then threatened M. de la Salle thought they would give him to us; this we desired because he lived near the Ohio. I asked the interpreter to speak to the Iroquois, but he soon told me the prisoner belonged to an old woman whose son had been killed, and that it would be impossible for us to prevent his death. I insisted, offering to pay any ransom asked; but the interpreter still refused to make the request, saying it would only place himself and us in danger, as the woman was related to the leading chiefs, and this Indian custom of expiation was one that even a chief dared not break."

The horrible details of the execution need not be given, but the reader can imagine what effect the tortures they witnessed had upon the party. M. Gallinée concludes his story thus:

"If I had known that they intended to kill him, I would have assuredly baptized him, because then I should have had the night in which to instruct him; but when the knowledge suddenly came a few moments before his sufferings began, I could only encourage him to bear it patiently and to offer his torments to God. I succeeded in making him understand better than I had hoped, because he knew the Algonquin tongue, which I could speak, and he said after me, and continued to repeat it during his sufferings: 'Thou who hast made all, have pity upon me.'

"I could only retire to our lodge full of grief that I could not save this poor captive, and better than ever I understood that it was wiser for me not to go among these nations without understanding their language, or being assured of an interpreter. M. de la Salle came in to say the excitement in the village made him apprehend further trouble. Many of the Indians were drunk, and they might insult us in such a manner that we should be forced into a difficulty with them, and that it would be better to return to the canoes, and to wait there with the rest of our people until the Indians became calm and sober. This good advice was acted upon, and we went to rejoin M. Dollier, about six leagues from the village. . . .

"During our stay in the village we had made many inquiries as to the route we should follow to arrive at the Ohio River, and every one had told us that by going in the canoes to the next lake we could land at a spot only three days' march from the head-waters of the river. The Indians had told our interpreter frightful stories of the tribes we would meet, saying when we reached the Ohio we would encounter a people who would certainly put us to death, and for that reason they had not given us a guide, for fear the governor would hold them responsible for what might happen to us. It was easy to see the interpreter was too frightened to be of any use.

"When our neighbors visited us after their fearful orgy was over, they put off the subject of a guide from day to day, and we saw we were losing the favorable season, and were uncertain as to where we could pass the winter. M. de la Salle said our death was assured if we should attempt to winter in the woods. We were relieved of this uneasiness by the arrival of one of the chiefs, who had returned from the council with the Dutch in New Holland. This Indian assured us there should be no difficulty about a guide; that he had captives from the different tribes where we desired to go, and he himself would very willingly go with us. Led by this hope, we quitted the Sonnontouans.

"Our guide took us to a river an eighth of a league in width, and extremely rapid, which brings the waters of the upper lakes into Lake Ontario. The depth of this river is something prodigious below where it falls from the upper lake through the grandest cataract in the world. The haste we were in to get to our landing place prevented our taking time to see this marvel. We had to make our portage from near the mouth of the river, some distance from the cataract, by a path the Indians knew, which led us around and above the rapids through which the waters pass before they fall over the cataract.

"While waiting at the little village below this place, where all the people were engaged to carry our baggage, M. de la Salle returned from a hunt, bringing back a severe attack of fever, which in a few days brought him very low.

"After three days of waiting, all the leading men of the village came to see us. At this council our Dutchman was of more use as an interpreter than he had been at the larger village of the Sonnontouans. There was another exchange of presents, and two captives were given us as guides, one of the tribe of the Chiouanons, the other of the Nez-Percés. The Chiouanon fell to M. de la Salle, and the other to us.

"We left this place with more than fifty savages and savagesses, and it took us two days to reach the end of the portage where our baggage was waiting. Here we learned that two Frenchmen were at the village to which we were going, who had come from the land of the Outaouacs, and on arriving at our destination on the 24th September, we found Sieur Jolliet, who had arrived the day before on his return from Lake Superior, where he had been sent by the governor to examine the newly discovered copper-mines.

"The illness of M. de la Salle had begun to take away his desire to go on to the Ohio, and now he began to be equally anxious to return to Montreal. The representations of Sieur Jolliet determined us to change our route, and visit the missions on the Superior, while M. de la Salle said the state of his health did not permit him to think of the journey to Lake Superior, and he begged us to excuse him for abandoning us on the way."

That the Abbé Gallinée did not understand La Salle is evident from the mention he makes of his illness, "caused by fright at meeting three rattlesnakes in the path."

M. Dollier, an ex-soldier, brought up in the school of Turenne, was a much better judge of the metal of the young comrade, who courteously pleaded the state of his health as a reason for turning back when the Abbé and M. Dollier changed their plan of going to the Ohio, and decided to visit the missions on the the upper lakes. La Salle's excuses made ("fine words," Dollier calls them), he left the two priests and their followers on the north side of Lake Ontario, and returned either to the Indian villages or to the south side of Niagara River, and continued his way thence to the Ohio. There is some doubt as to the route he followed, but none as to his determined purpose and its accomplishment. Unfortunately, the papers and maps which record the journey, and illustrate the course pursued, and which were in the possession of his niece in 1756, were lost in the later years of that stormy century.

A Memoir of La Salle, written by one of his contemporaries (supposed to be the Abbé Renaudot), gives a condensed sketch of the trip, as La Salle told it to the writer; it is geographically correct and indisputably true, and therefore is added herewith:—

"M. de la Salle went back to the Indian village, and from thence started anew to find the Ohio. The Indians guided him across by easy portages to the head-waters of the Ohio; after reaching that river he pursued his journey westward until he came to the rapids, which end in a low swampy country. Here he was constrained to land; leaving the river for the higher ridges (on the northern bank) he found an Indian-hunting camp. These Indians told him that some distance below the river, which here seemed to have lost itself in little rivulets that wandered about through the vast extent of forest-covered marshes, reunited its waters in a great stream. This decided him to continue his journey by land; but that night his followers deserted him, and, regaining the river above the rapids, went back.

"Finding himself alone (except for one or two faithful Indians), and over four hundred leagues from Montreal, he could do nothing, but return."

The official records of THE DISCOVERY OF THE RIVER yet rest in the French Archives, and are shown in three or four documents which are reproduced in M. Margry's late work.

First. There is a petition to the king ("Demande du Privilege"), asking certain concessions in recognition of his discoveries south of the lakes, and especially of the Ohio River.

Second. There are the official maps, made (by his rivals) in 1673 and the years immediately following, which show the course of the Ohio, and in each the discovery is credited to La Salle.

Third. There are several dispatches to the king and to Colbert from the governor-general and intendant of Canada, in which mention is made of "these discoveries of Le Sieur de la Salle, of various countries and rivers south of the lakes;" and in each something is said of "the Beautiful River," which is called "The Ohio," "the Bright River," "the Shining River," and "the Deep Shining River."

Fourth. In consideration of his discoveries, the king grants him a patent of nobility, creating him a knight, and making him governor of Fort Frontenac.

An extract from one of these documents, in which La Salle speaks of himself in the third person, and the record ends:—

"In 1667, and the following years, he made many journeys—at great expense—in which he was the first discoverer of the country south of the Great Lakes, and among other rivers, the Ohio. He followed its current to the rapids, where, after having been increased by a large river coming from the north, it spreads over wide swampy lowlands; and there is every indication that these collected waters find their way to the Gulf of Mexico."

The other documents relating to La Salle in this new revelation of history belong to the records of the Mississippi.

EARLY DAYS ON "THE SHINING RIVER."

CHAPTER III.

FRENCH AND ENGLISH CONTEST FOR THE OHIO.

THE French, by right of La Salle's discovery, laid claim to the whole stretch of country from the great lakes to the Ohio, while England declared the territory to be hers, and had included it in her grant to the colony of Virginia. Each contestant had allies among the Indians, who, however, were from time to time easily influenced to desert the one and aid the other.

Toward the middle of the eighteenth century the white settlements in Virginia and Pennsylvania were reaching out to and extending over the mountain chain. Hunters and traders, the early pioneers of civilization, had brought back to the settlements upon every return from the Indian country highly colored reports of the richness of the Western mountain glades, and of the beauty and importance of the mountain streams, which they had already begun to connect with the stories that had come from the far South of the mystic and mighty Mississippi.

At this juncture Thomas Lee, one of the council of Virginia, organized a syndicate of London merchants, which was called THE OHIO COMPANY.* The object of the syndicate was to settle the wild lands south and west of the Ohio, and secure as large a part as possible of Indian trade from the French. This grant embraced a large area on the south of the Ohio, between the Monongahela and Kanawha Rivers, with the further privilege of taking such lands on the north side of the river as should subsequently be deemed expedient. This territory was exempt

---
* Appendix A, No. II.

from taxation on condition of its being taken up by actual settlers within a limited time, and also that the company should build a fort and sustain a garrison for their protection. To gain the good-will of the Indians a treaty was proposed, and that no time might be lost the company resolved to open roads from the head-waters of the Potomac to some convenient point on the Monongahela.

That Pennsylvania might not be distanced in the race, the proprietary government through Andrew Palmer, president of the council, gave instructions, January 23, 1748, to their agent to use his utmost diligence to visit all the neighboring tribes, and learn their numbers, strength, and disposition toward the colony. Their agent, Weiser, had one eminent advantage over his compeers; he knew perfectly the language of the people with whom he was empowered to open negotiations. He immediately started West, and received invaluable aid from George Crogan, a trader and agent of the proprietary council, who was already settled on Beaver Creek, a few miles from its junction with the Ohio.

Unhappily neither the government of Pennsylvania nor the attempts of the OHIO COMPANY, under the patronage of the council of VIRGINIA, succeeded in conciliating the disaffected Indians, or in dividing them from the French, who had already begun to build a line of forts from their settlements in Canada to the outlet of the Mississippi below New Orleans. Their northern forts were situated at Presque Isle on Lake Erie, at Le Bœuf, and at Venango. The building of these forts so aroused the spirit of the English that Governor Dinwiddie, of Virginia, sent Washington to the French commander at Le Bœuf to demand his "reasons for invading English territory in time of peace." On November 22, 1753, the "young envoy" reached Frazier's, at the mouth of Turtle Creek; from thence he continued his route by way of Hill's Creek to Shannopin's, an old Indian town on the Allegheny, about two miles above its union with the Monongahela. He examined the position at the junction of the affluents forming the Ohio, and reported the point as favorable for a fortification. At Logstown he called together a council of Indians, and although he gained the information he sought relative to the French garrisons and numbers, he was constantly thwarted by the influence the French had gained over the Indians. He proceeded to Le Bœuf, where he delivered his dispatches to the French commander, who in reply to the message from the governor of Virginia said that "it was not in his province to specify the evidence and demonstrate the right of the king, his master, to the lands situated on the Ohio, but he would transmit the letter to the Marquis du Quesne, and act according to the answer he should receive from that nobleman."* He did not hesitate to declare, however, that in the meantime he should "hold all the land claimed through the discovery of La Salle." With this unqualified statement, Washington set out on his return, encountering on the way many hardships and perils. Much of the journey from Venango was made on foot with a single companion. Once he barely escaped death by drowning; again he was shot at by an Indian, at a distance of but fifteen paces, yet received no injury. Although impatient at every delay, he spent a whole day, with the aid of a poor hatchet, in constructing a rude raft on which to cross the Allegheny; but he soon found himself blocked in the ice, and unable to proceed until the river was completely frozen over. Rapid progress at such a season

---

*The letter from the governor of Virginia required the French to withdraw from the dominions of Great Britain.

was impossible; but at last he arrived with his dispatches safe in Williamsburg.

In spite of ill reports brought by Washington from their western domains, the Ohio Company decided to strengthen their position in the west. They had one block-house at Redstone (now Brownsville), and they determined to take and hold permanent posession of the entire country named in their grant. In February, 1754, they sent a re-enforcement and began the foundation of a redoubt where Pittsburg now stands. Before the work was finished Contrecœur, a French officer, with one thousand French and Indians, and eighteen pieces of cannon, arrived from Venango, and compelled the surrender of the post, which they fortified and named Fort Duquesne, after the governor of Canada. They loaded their Indian allies with presents of guns, ammunition, blankets, and beads, and the joy of conquest completed the alienation of the Indians from the English, and the treaty of 1754 was made.

On his return from the French forts Washington had been placed in command of an expedition to aid in completing the redoubt begun by his advice. *En route* for this point he had reached Will's Creek (afterwards Fort Cumberland), when he learned of Contrecœur's descent upon the redoubt. Nothing daunted, he wrote to the governor for re-enforcements, and determined to push on to the Monongahela. His plan was to wait at Redstone for Colonel Fry's troops on their retreat from the lost position, then drop down the river and attack the French. But he had not accomplished more than fifty miles through this rough country when he was apprised by a dispatch from the half-king* of the approach of the enemy. He was

---

* A title given to one of the Shawnee chiefs.

encamped at Great Meadows, where he now determined to intrench himself. After sending out reconnoitering parties, who failed to discover any trace of the French, Washington, with forty men, set out at nine o'clock on a dark and rainy night, and by difficult and toilsome paths, reached the half-king's camp at sunrise. His Indian ally knew where the tracks of the French had been seen, and consented to send two of his people to follow these tracks to the lurking-place of the enemy, while expressing his willingness to go hand in hand with his brother, as he called Washington, to strike the French. The result was an engagement of about fifteen minutes, in which the French were defeated. Their party had come as spies, but pretended to have been sent with a communication to Washington, who, however, was not deluded by the excuse. Sending his prisoners, twenty-one in number, to Governor Dinwiddie, at Williamsburg, he prepared for the attack which he had good reason to expect, and Fort Necessity* was hastily strengthened. On the 3d of July it was attacked by seven hundred French and Indians. The fight lasted for nine hours. The courage of the raw provincials and the coolness of their young leader enabled them to hold the position against greatly superior numbers. The French commander, De Villiers, sent in a flag of truce, offering terms of capitulation, which were accepted. The English withdrew from their only foothold upon the Ohio; and the Beautiful River, together with the entire valley of the Mississippi, was left to the French and their Indian allies.

The next effort to regain Fort Duquesne was part of the well planned and badly executed campaign of 1755. A large

---

* Fort Necessity was eight miles from Uniontown, on the Youghiogheny, and about fifty miles from Cumberland.

and well-disciplined army, under General Braddock, was to storm the fort, and wrest the Ohio Valley from the French.

"After taking Fort Duquesne," Braddock said to Franklin, "I am to proceed to Niagara, and having taken that, to Frontenac. Duquesne can hardly detain me more than three or four days, and then I can see nothing that can obstruct my march to Niagara."

"The Indians are dexterous in laying and executing ambuscades," suggested Franklin.

"The savages may be formidable to your raw American militia; upon the king's regular and well-disciplined troops it is impossible they should make any impression," replied the British general.

After numerous delays, Braddock succeeded in marching his army across the mountains to within ten miles of Fort Duquesne. The French, aware of his approach, with the aid of the Indians sallied forth to prepare an ambuscade. They unexpectedly found themselves in the presence of the English, and instantly began an attack, which lasted for two hours, and resulted most disastrously for Braddock's regulars, who were terrified by the yells of the Indians, and utterly demoralized from the first. Washington, acting as aid to General Braddock, was in the thickest of the fight, and his escape seemed almost miraculous. Braddock fell mortally wounded, after having had five horses killed under him. He was carried off the field on a stretcher made of his heavy sash, to a place of safety; but died before the retreating army reached Cumberland. The English lost seven hundred killed and wounded; while of the French and Indians only thirty-three were killed. The defeated army was not pursued, as the Indians could not be induced to leave the scene of carnage.

Three years passed before any further effort was made to dislodge the French from the "Gateway of the West." Fortunately for the Colonies England now had a minister who recognized the importance of the position. Pitt determined the English to make fresh effort to obtain possession of Fort Duquesne. An expedition for this purpose was intrusted to General Joseph Forbes, who, after long waiting and many disappointments, found himself at the head of an army of six thousand two hundred men—Scotch Highlanders, Royal Americans, Militia, and Volunteers; among the last were Benjamin West, the painter, and Anthony Wayne, then a lad of thirteen. Washington, in command of the Virginia regiments, led the advance, and but for him the expedition would most probably have failed. During the long and trying march through snow and over rocky roads his brave spirit cheered his men, and made them disregard hardships which they would not have borne so uncomplainingly under a leader less trusted.

The garrison at Fort Duquesne, disheartened at the approach of so superior a force, determined to abandon the post. Accordingly, after setting fire to the fort on the night of November 24, 1758, they embarked on the river in the light of the flames. On the evening of the next day the British flag floated over the ruins, and from that time the place has commemorated the name of Pitt.

The possession of the Ohio was now secured by the English; and the contest between two civilized nations for land, rightfully the property of neither, was ended.

THREE HUNDRED FEET UP BLACKWATER.

Chapter IV.

EARLY SETTLEMENTS.

THE earliest settlements on the Ohio River were made in the years 1770 and 1773—the one by the Zane brothers, at Wheeling; the other at Louisville, by the Taylors, Thomas Bullitt, the McAfees, McCouns, and Adams.

The spot selected by the Zanes in 1769 became in 1777 the scene of the memorable siege of Fort Henry, in which a little band of defenders were opposed by savages more than thirty times their number, led by Simon Girty, the renegade.

After fighting for several hours the supply of powder was so reduced that a surrender would have been inevitable but for the heroism of Elizabeth Zane. At her brother's house, across an open space just outside the fort, was a keg of gunpowder, to obtain which the commander was about to send out one of the men, when the sister of the Zanes stepped forward and insisted that to her the undertaking should be intrusted, urging that the danger attending the venture was sufficient reason why the life of a soldier should not be risked, for the garrison was already too weak to spare even one of its number. The firing was discontinued for a short time, thus giving a favorable opportunity to the brave girl, who, in full view of the enemy, made her way across the open space, obtained her prize, and was returning with it before the Indians suspected her purpose. They immediately leveled their pieces and aimed a volley at her as she ran toward the gate; but not a ball grazed her clothing, and she entered the fort in safety, bearing the keg of powder in her arms.

Although the spot upon which Louisville was built was selected in 1773, it was an uncertain home for the few families there collected, who were in constant dread of the Indians. All this was changed in 1778, when George Rogers Clark made his successful foray into the Indian country. Virginia had raised a regiment for the defense of the western frontier; with this force Clark descended the Monongahela and the Ohio to the Falls.* Halting a few days at the little settlement, he waited for the Kentucky volunteers to join him. One direct consequence of his success was the preservation of the settlement at the mouth of "Bear Grass Creek." Previous to that period the families of the pioneers who were collected at the Falls of the Ohio had been compelled to seek safety upon the small island abreast of the present site of the city. Here Clark had built a fort, and at his departure about thirteen families remained on this narrow islet, in the midst of the foaming rapids, surrounded by enemies and enduring the severest privations, yet tenaciously maintaining their foothold. The capture of Vincennes, by breaking up the nearest and strongest of the enemy's western posts, relieved their apprehensions of immediate danger, and encouraged them to settle permanently on the Kentucky shore.

The possibility of establishing settlements on the river having been demonstrated at the two points mentioned, it was not long before other bands of determined men were induced, either by the love of adventure or the fertility of the soil, to brave the hardships and dangers of pioneer life. A clear title to four hundred acres of well-watered and well-timbered productive land, in an agreeable

---
* Appendix A, No. III.

EARLY SETTLEMENTS.

climate, where game was abundant, could be obtained by simply putting up a log cabin and raising *one* crop. For this reason many a hardy woodsman of the older settlements, where land was both poor in quality and high in price, made light of the risk; and thinking only of gain, shouldered his rifle and ax, and with all his wordly goods on a pack-saddle, made his way, with horse and dog, over the mountains.

Wild and extravagant stories were wafted across the Atlantic. Designing agents of more designing speculators formed in France a company of five hundred emigrants, who left their native shores and encountered perils by sea and land to reach the "wonderful Ohio Valley." They landed at Alexandria, but it was months before their conductors made arrangements for them to cross the mountains. After having been two years on the journey they reached their destination, and began building the town of Gallipolis, on the Ohio River.*

About the same time settlements were begun at Marietta, Manchester, Maysville, and Cincinnati, in spite of the outrages committed by the savages. Accounts of inhuman butcheries and cruel tortures inflicted upon the early settler fill pages of history. Strong men, bravely patient women, innocent children, all learned to dread the savage yell which announced the presence of the Indian; and they feared still more the treacherous ambuscade into which, when in apparent security, so many heedlessly wandered. Homes were destroyed, the husband and father slain and scalped, the wife and mother carried into captivity, and little children tomahawked and left to feed the wild beasts that lurked in the forests bordering the "Warrior's Road." An incident in the history of Maysville will give a

---
*Appendix A, No. IV.

very fair picture of what might be looked for by those attempting to settle on the river:

"John May and several companions were drifting down the Ohio, bound for Maysville, when suddenly, at daylight one morning, an alarm of danger was given. A dense smoke was seen rising above the trees on the northern shore. The party determined at once to seek the opposite side of the river; but they were hailed by two white men, who ran down to the shore and implored to be taken on board. They said that they had just escaped from the Indians, and were closely pursued, and unless taken on board would surely be recaptured and killed. They were suspected of treachery by some of the party in the boat, but their entreaties made others beg that they might be rescued. May was resolute in his refusal, but one of his companions induced him to put in to the shore just long enough to allow him to land. The savages hidden under the drooping willows were instantly masters of the situation, though they contented themselves for some time with firing upon the crew without making any attempt to take possession of the boat. As soon as it was seen that resistance was useless, all hands lay down on their faces wherever they could best be protected. One of the women was shot and instantly killed, one of the men was severely wounded, and May, finding the firing hotter at every moment, waved a signal of surrender, and was killed in the act. The savages now made for the boat, and on boarding it shook hands with their prisoners, and then coolly scalped the dead. After pulling the boat ashore they examined and destroyed every thing of value, until they stumbled upon a keg of whisky, which they carried off in great exultation. . . .

"One of their captives was burned at the stake; another, after running the gauntlet, was condemned to death, but made his escape. A woman of the party who had seen her sister shot and killed, had been bound to the stake, fagots were piled around her ready to be fired, when a chief, more merciful than his companions, interfered and had her released."

It was amid scenes such as these that the settlements on the Ohio River were begun, and notwithstanding the frequent raids of the savages the number of these settlements steadily increased, until the whole region was reclaimed; for the Red Man learned to

EARLY SETTLEMENTS.

dread the "Long Knives," and prudently withdrew to other hunting-grounds. The attractions of the country were so varied, and the Indians had been so thoroughly taught to respect the fighting qualities of the Scotch-Irish emigrants from the valley of Virginia and Pennsylvania, that we can understand why Washington said of the settlement at Marietta: "No colony was ever settled under more favorable auspices."

Glowing accounts were sent back to their old homes by the "advance guard" of civilization—they were enthusiastic about the riches of the Ohio country, "where cattle could be fed all the year round on pasturage springing spontaneously from the soil; where lands suitable for raising grain could outvie the islands of the Mediterranean; and where there were bogs from which might be gathered cranberries enough to make tarts for all New England."

The other side of the picture was passed over in silence; no mention was made of danger and discomfort, of crops wantonly destroyed by vengeful Indians, of flocks robbed by wild animals, of the inconvenience of being farmer and soldier at once; for no man dared venture from his door without a rifle, and guards were invariably posted to give an alarm to those working in the field should there be any sign of the enemy.

These delusive accounts sent by the pioneers to friends in their old homes awakened the keenest interest, and soon new re-enforcements poured into the settlements from New England, Pennsylvania, and Virginia. The old Braddock trail became one of the highways by which the emigrant sought his new home, and on reaching an affluent of the Ohio a flat-boat was constructed, and the journey continued. These boats, called keels, sometimes "from fifty to seventy-five feet long, were sharp at both ends, drawing little water, and capable of carrying a good burden."*

The more provident man, of those seeking homes in the western wilds, always preceded his family, and spent a season in raising a crop and in other preparations, before making the move; otherwise much suffering was often the result, for when the supply of provisions brought from across the mountains was exhausted, it could only be replenished with game. Lean venison and the breast of wild turkey were substituted for bread, and bear's-flesh or other gross food was styled meat. After a season's crops had been gathered the family bill of fare ordinarily consisted of "hog and hominy," with Johnny-cake for breakfast and dinner, and mush for supper. This last was frequently served and eaten with bear's oil, *à l'Indienne.*

Crockery was an unheard-of luxury; wooden trenchers and much-battered pewter ware, supplemented with bone or gourd, were considered luxuries. Iron utensils and knives and forks, as well as salt and iron castings, were brought across the mountains on pack-horses, and were consequently very expensive.

A caravan trade was carried on in order to obtain indispensables, but furs and peltries were the only articles of export until time enough had elapsed for the raising of cattle and horses for Eastern markets. A cow and calf was the usual price paid for a bushel of salt, which, until weights came into use, was meas-

---

* Other boats then in use were called arks: "These arks are built for sale for the accommodation of families descending the river, and for the convenience of produce. They are flat-bottomed and square at the ends, and are all made of the same dimensions, being fifty feet long and fourteen broad. They are covered, and are managed by a steering-oar, which can be lifted out of the water. The usual price is seventy-five dollars, and each will accommodate three or four families as they carry from twenty-five to thirty tons."—*Bradbury.*

ured by hand into a half bushel. This was done with the utmost care, and every precaution taken to prevent the displacement of a single grain.

Each family possessed a hominy-block, which consisted of a huge block of wood with a hole burnt in one end, and so formed that the pestle would throw the corn in such a manner as to make it fall back into the center, and thus come again under the strokes of the pestle. The hand-mill, usually possessed by several families in common, was precisely the same as that used in Palestine to-day, and which is mentioned in the Bible. It was made of two circular stones placed in a hoop, with a spout for sending off the meal. A handle was fitted in the upper stone, and so fastened that two persons could grind at the same time; the grain was run by hand into the opening in the upper stone. The first water-mills were called tub-mills, and were of very simple construction. Instead of bolting-cloths, sifters of deer-skins were used; these were made by stretching the skin in a state of parchment over a hoop, and perforating it with a hot wire.

Homespun and home-cut garments alone were used, linsey-woolsey—a mixture of flax and wool—and coarse linen were the staple fabrics. It was not until the first retail store was opened at Louisville, in 1783, that the belle of the "forest land" could adorn her comely person in gorgeous calico, and the dandy of the settlement could doff his coon-skin cap for a wool hat. A chronicler of the day, in commenting on this store, says: "The tone of society became visibly more elevated."

In building his cabin the settler had no use for other tools than an ax, an augur, and a cross-cut saw. Wooden pins took the place of nails, and unhewn logs, poles, clapboards, and puncheons were the materials necessary. If a window were desired, the aperture was fitted with a frame, over which oiled paper was stretched; but light was usually admitted through the open door. When in the course of time an enterprising merchant added window-glass to his stock in trade, and by way of advertising his new commodity improved his own establishment, great was the amazement of the settlement urchins, who had never seen any other habitation than that of the backwoodsman. One of the hopefuls, on seeing for the first time a house with glass windows, rushed home to his mother, exclaiming: "O, ma, there is a house down here with specs on."

A hard life of constant toil in the midst of ever-present danger admitted few opportunities for merry-making. Log-rolling, cabin-building, and harvesting always ended with a frolic, but the celebration of a marriage was the sole occasion when friends met for pleasure alone. Wedding festivities sometimes continued for several days; they were always initiated at the house of the groom, where his attendants met to accompany him to the home of the bride. The party would set out in great glee, but their progress would frequently be interrupted by barricades of grape-vines. Practical jokes of various kinds met them at every turn, until, when within a mile of their destination, the race for "Black Betty" began. Two of the party being selected by the others, put their ponies to their utmost speed, and the one reaching the house first received at the door a bottle of whisky, with which he returned to treat the groom and his attendants.

The marriage always took place in the forenoon, and dinner followed immediately after the ceremony. Then came the dancing, invariably beginning with a "square four," which led into what was called "jigging it off," and was kept up without intermission for hours.

Although the standard of morals was generally good, but few—before the days of camp-meetings, which, however, were early instituted—regarded Sunday other than a rest-day for the aged and a play-day for the youngster. But if religion was wanting, superstition abounded, and many held firmly to a belief in witches.*

In one of the settlements drunkenness had become so distressing the better class of the community determined to try to abate the evil by imposing a fine; the stumps had not yet been removed from the public thoroughfares, and it was decreed that any person found guilty of intemperance should be compelled to dig up a stump. The plan worked admirably. But some of the fines and penalties, though assigned by a judge of the court, were sometimes quite disproportionate to the offense; in more than one instance an offender was condemned to death for petty larceny.

The price at which certain articles might be sold was fixed by court: A half-pint of whisky at $15; corn at $10 a gallon; lodging in a feather-bed, $6; a "diet," $12; and stable or pasturage for one night, $4. The seeming exorbitance of these charges is accounted for by the fact that Continental money was the only currency.

In the first days of a settlement but little attention was paid to drainage, and of the many disorders prevalent in consequence, perhaps rheumatism was most general; for this reason each

---

* It was often said that witches had milked the cows, and this was supposed to have been done, "by fixing a new pin in a new towel for each cow intended to be milked; the towel was hung over her own door, and by means of certain incantations the witch extracted milk from the fringes of the towel after the manner of milking a cow."

backwoodsman slept with his feet to the fire, either to prevent or to allay the trouble. The sovereign remedy for this and other diseases was "Seneca Oil," the petroleum of the present day.*

Perhaps there is nothing more amazing in the development of the country than the rapidity with which manufacturing establishments sprang up, first on its southern affluents, and then on the Ohio itself. Before the close of the century (which had entered its eighth decade when the first step was made towards civilizing the Ohio region) flour was shipped in considerable quantities for New Orleans and the West Indies, in vessels built on the Allegheny or Monongahela; and glass-houses, paper-mills, rope-walks, tanneries, potteries, powder-mills, salt-works,† and printing-offices were in operation at various points.

At the close of the century the river began to present a very lively appearance. Up to 1795 the population numbered not more than twenty-five families for each hundred miles of the river's length, from Pittsburgh to its mouth; but by 1802 plantations were said to have increased so "that they were not more than from one to three miles asunder, and some of them always within sight from the middle of the river."‡ Perhaps this statement had best be taken *cum grano salis*; but the influx from Pennsylvania and Virginia had undoubtedly made a marked difference in the prosperity of the settlements. Arks were con-

---

*"The Seneca Indian Oil is a liqiud bitumen which oozes through fissures of the rocks, and is found floating on the surface of several springs."—*Harris's Tour.*

"Here is a spring on the top of which floats an oil similar to that called Barbadoes tar. It is very efficacious in rheumatic pains; troops sent to guard the Western posts bathed their joints with it, and found great relief from rheumatic complaints with which they were afflicted."—*Navigator.*

† "That the Indians were acquainted with the art of evaporating salt-brine, is evident from the ancient pottery found near the Kanawha salt-works."—*Dodge.*

‡ Michaux.

stantly passing down the river, transporting human freight, as well as live-stock, farming implements, and such articles as were deemed indispensable to the establishment of a home in the wilderness.

Pittsburgh had gained in commercial what it had lost in military importance. It had been transformed from a well-guarded outpost, with a few straggling huts built near the fortification, to a town of four hundred houses (many of which were of brick), and the fort adjoining the town had sunk into insignificance, and was manned only by a weak garrison, for the Indians had now withdrawn into the interior. The town could boast of two printing-offices and four newspapers a week, and had become the entrepôt for goods shipped at Philadelphia for the western settlements, as well as for the products that were sent to New Orleans from the towns on the Allegheny and Monongahela, and the surrounding country. Some of these articles were flour, hams, smoked pork, bar iron, coarse cloths, bottles, whisky, and barreled butter. Three-masted vessels of two hundred tons burthen were being constructed; others of considerable tonnage had already been launched on the Monongahela. They were supplied with cordage manufactured at Redstone (Brownsville).

Wheeling, Marietta, Cincinnati, Maysville, Manchester, Carrollton, and Louisville had grown in proportion to the location and the character of their settlers and those of the adjacent country, among whom were many who preferred the excitement of the chase to the plodding life of a tiller of the soil. The hardships, trials, and vexations the early settlers endured with patience and courage can not easily be appreciated by a people who are looking backward through the vista of a century.

More resolute, honest, and upright men have never opened

a country for the coming of civilization, than were the settlers who builded their rough log cabins upon the forest-clad banks of the Monongahela. The women who shared their checkered fortunes were worthy to be the wives and mothers of those hardy, daring pioneers of a republic which owes its existence to their fortitude and courage, and its greatness to their virtue and patriotism.

These settlers had followed in the wake of the "long hunters" of Virginia and Western Pennsylvania. Their homes were hospitably open to all travelers, and the "block-houses" were rallying-points for Indian traders and Indian fighters, before the Colonies refused to drink taxed tea, or unfurled the Starry Flag in the teeth of every wind that blew.

In every struggle west of the mountains, where men were hastily gathered by hundreds or twenties, to fight French troops and their Indian allies, or, in later days, English and Indian invaders, the pioneers met the shock and brunt of battle. Wherever danger stalked or border foes met in desperate encounter, the courage of the settlers was tested, and, in the main, it rang true as steel. They were restive under military restraint, for they were above all things FREEMEN, accustomed to the freedom of the woods; but as trailers of a predatory foe—ready to endure fatigue, hunger, physical suffering, careless of wounds, careless of death—they were matchless. They were no less ready to dare any and all odds, in hand-to-hand fights, upon "The Shining River;" or under the lintels of their cabins, if a little band of daring warriors crept past the frontier forts, to strike these outlying farms, and gather the blood-red trophies which were to give them rank in the tribes.

In the record of individual daring, Wheeling has commem-

EARLY SETTLEMENTS. 75

orated a gallant deed by naming the bluff above Wheeling Creek *McCulloch's Leap.*

In September of 1782 Fort Henry was besieged by some five hundred Indians, commanded by Simon Girty, who figures in the history of the time as a renegade more cruel than the Indians he led. In the history of the relief of the garrison, this incident is given:

"About daybreak Major Samuel McCulloch, with forty mounted men from Short Creek, came to the relief of the little garrison. The gate was thrown open, and McCulloch's men, though closely beset by the Indians, entered in safety, but McCulloch himself was not permitted to pass the gateway; the Indians crowded around him and separated him from his party. After several ineffectual attempts to force his way to the gate, he wheeled about and galloped with the swiftness of a deer in the direction of Wheeling Hill.

"The Indians might easily have killed him, but they cherished towards him an almost frenzied hatred; for he had participated in so many encounters that almost every warrior personally knew him. To take him alive, and glut their full revenge by the most fiendish tortures, was their object, and they made almost superhuman exertions to capture him. He put spurs to his horse and soon became completely hemmed in on three sides, and the fourth was almost a perpendicular precipice of one hundred and fifty feet descent, with Wheeling Creek at its base. Supporting his rifle on his left hand, and carefully adjusting his reins with the other, he urged his horse to the brink of the bluff, and then made the leap which decided his fate. The next moment the noble steed, still bearing his intrepid rider in safety, was at the foot of the precipice. McCulloch immediately dashed across the creek and was soon beyond the reach of the Indians.

"After the escape of Major McCulloch the Indians concentrated at the foot of the hill, and soon after set fire to all the houses and fences outside of the fort, and killed about three hundred head of cattle belonging to the settlers. They then raised the siege and took up the line of march to some other theater of action.

"As the reader will very naturally desire to learn the fate of Major McCulloch after his almost miraculous escape from the Indians, some account of the manner of his death may be properly introduced in this place.

"Not long after the siege of Fort Henry, indications of Indians having been noticed by some of the settlers, Major McCulloch and his brother John mounted their horses and left Van Metre's fort to ascertain the correctness of the report. They crossed Short Creek, and continued in the direction of Wheeling, but inclining towards the river. They scouted closely, but cautiously, and not discovering any such 'signs' as had been stated, descended to the river bottom at a point on the farm subsequently owned by Alfred P. Woods, about two miles above Wheeling. They then passed up the river to the mouth of Short Creek, and thence up Girty's Point in the direction of Van Metre's. Not discovering any indications of the enemy, the brothers were riding leisurely along, when, a short distance beyond the 'Point,' a deadly discharge of rifles took place, killing Major Samuel McCulloch instantly. His brother John escaped, but his horse was killed. Immediately mounting that of his brother he made off to give the alarm. As yet no enemy had been seen; but, turning in his saddle after riding fifty yards, the path was filled with Indians, and one fellow was seen in the act of scalping the unfortunate major. Quick as thought the rifle of John was at his shoulder; an instant later and the savage was rolling in the agonies of death. John escaped to the fort unhurt, with the exception of a slight wound of his hip.

"On the following day a party of men from Van Metre's went out and gathered up the mutilated remains of Major McCulloch. The savages had disemboweled him, but the viscera all remained except the *heart*. Some years subsequent to this melancholy affair, an Indian, who had been one of the party on this occasion, told some whites that the heart of Major McCulloch had been divided and *eaten by the party*. 'This was done,' said he, 'that we be bold, like Major McCulloch.'"

To define the times it is necessary to insist upon the fact that the "Law of the Border" was the *law of retaliation*. The incident just given, and the crime chronicled here, are proofs which show *both* sides of this *question*.

"The Moravian Indians consisted chiefly of Delawares and Mohicans, who had been converted to Christianity through the zeal and influence of the Moravian missionaries. They had four towns on the Upper Muskingum, in the line of travel between the nearest point on the Ohio River and Upper Sandusky, the home of the Delawares and other warlike tribes. The Moravian Indians were always friendly toward the whites. During the whole of the Revolutionary War they had remained neutral, or if they took part, it was in favor of the Americans, advising them of the approach of hostile Indians, and rendering other kindly offices. For ten years of border strife they had lived in peace and quietness, but at length became objects of suspicion to both whites and savages. They were, it may be said, between two fires. While passing to and fro, the hostile parties would *compel* them to furnish provisions. It is not surprising, therefore, that they should have fallen a sacrifice to one or the other.

"It happened that early in February, 1782, a party of Indians from Sandusky penetrated the white settlements and committed numerous depredations. Of the families which fell beneath the murderous stroke of these savages was that of David Wallace, consisting of himself, wife, and six children, and at the same time a man named Carpenter was taken prisoner. The early date of this visitation induced the whites to believe that the depredators had wintered with the Moravians, and they at once resolved on executing summary vengeance. About the 1st of March a body of eighty or ninety men gathered at Mingo Bottom, a few miles below the present town of Steubenville, Ohio. The second day's march brought them within a short distance of one of the Moravian towns (of which there were four), and they encamped for the night.

"The victims received warning of their danger, but took no measures to escape, believing that they had nothing to fear from the Americans. On the arrival of an advanced party of sixteen men they professed peace and good-will to the Moravians, and informed them that they had come to take them to Fort Pitt for safety. The Indians surrendered, delivering up their arms, even their hatchets, on being promised that everything should be restored to them on their arrival at Pittsburg. By persuasion of some and driving of others, the inhabitants of two or three of the towns had been brought together and bound without resistance. A council of war was then held to decide their fate. The commandant, Colonel David Williamson, at the suggestion of his officers, then put the question to his men in form, "Whether the Moravian Indians should be taken prisoners to Pittsburg or put to death?" and requested that all who were in favor of saving their lives should step out of the line, and form a second rank. On this sixteen men stepped out, and formed themselves into a second line. The fearful determination of putting the Moravians to death was thus shown.

"Most of those opposed to this diabolical resolution protested in the name of high Heaven against the atrocious act, and called God to witness that they were innocent of the blood of these people; yet the majority remained unmoved, and some of them were even in favor of burning them alive. But it was at length decided that they should be scalped in cold blood, and the Indians were told to prepare for their fate. They were led into buildings, in one of which the men, and in the other the women and children, were confined like sheep for the slaughter. They passed the night in praying and exhorting one another, and singing hymns of praise to God.

"When the morning arrived for the purpose of slaughter, two houses were selected, one for the men and the other for the women and children. The victims were then bound two and two together, led into the slaughter-houses, and there scalped and murdered. The number of the slain, according to the Moravian account (for many of them had made their escape), was ninety-six. Of these, sixty-two were grown persons, one-third of whom were women; the remaining thirty-four were children.

"After the work of death had been finished and the plunder secured, all the buildings in the towns were set on fire. A rapid retreat to the settlements concluded this deplorable campaign."

"In justice to the memory of Colonel Williamson," says Doddridge, "I have to say, that although at that time very young, I was personally acquainted with him, and from my recollection of his conversation, I say, with confidence, that he was a brave man, but not cruel. He would meet an enemy in battle and fight like a soldier, but not murder a prisoner. Had he possessed the authority of a superior officer in a regular army, I do not believe that a single Moravian Indian would have lost his life; but he possessed no such authority. He was only a militia officer, who could advise, but not command. His only fault was that of too easy compliance with popular opinion and popular prejudice. On this account his memory has been loaded with unmerited reproach.

"Should it be asked, What sort of people composed this band of murderers? I answer, they were not all miscreants or vagabonds; many of them were men of the first standing in the country. Many of them had recently lost relations by the hands of the savage, and were burning with

EARLY SETTLEMENTS. 79

revenge. They cared little on whom they wreaked their vengeance, so they were Indians.

"When attacked by our people, although the Moravians might have defended themselves, they did not. They never fired a single shot. They were prisoners, and had been promised protection. Every dictate of justice required that their lives should be spared. It was, therefore, an atrocious and unqualified murder."

"The object of the campaign which succeeded was twofold: First, to complete the work of murdering and plundering the Moravians at their new establishment on the Sandusky; and secondly, to destroy the Wyandot towns on the same river. It was the resolution of all concerned in this expedition not to spare the life of any Indian that might fall into their hands, friend or foe, man, woman, or child. But, as will be seen in the sequel, the result was widely different from that of the Moravian campaign of the preceding March.

"It would seem that the long continuance of this Indian war had greatly demoralized the early settlers, and being prompted by an indiscriminate thirst for revenge, they were prepared to go to almost any extreme of barbarity.

"On the 25th of May, 1782, four hundred and eighty men mustered at Mingo Bottom and preceeded to elect their commander. The choice fell upon Colonel William Crawford, who accepted the command with some degree of reluctance.

"The army marched along 'Williamson's Trail,' until they arrived at the ruins of the upper Moravian town, in the fields, belonging to which there was still plenty of corn on the stalks, with which their horses were fed during the night.

"Shortly after the army halted at this place, two Indians were discovered by some men who had walked out of the camp. Three shots were fired at one of them, but without effect. As soon as the news reached the camp, more than one-half of the men rushed out, without command, and in the most tumultuous manner, to see what had happened. From that time Colonel Crawford felt a presentiment of the defeat which followed.

"The truth is, that notwithstanding the secrecy and dispatch with which the enterprise had been gotten up, the Indians were beforehand with the whites. They saw the rendezvous on the Mingo Bottom, and knew the number and destination of the troops. They visited every encampment immediately after the troops had left, and saw from their writing on the trees and scraps of paper that 'no quarter' was to be given to any Indian, whether man, woman, or child.

"Nothing of importance happened during their march until the 6th of June, when their guide conducted them to the site of the Moravian villages on one of the upper branches of the Sandusky River. From this retreat the Christian Indians had lately been driven away by the Wyandots to the Scioto, and here the army of Colonel Crawford, instead of finding Indians and plunder, met with nothing but vestiges of ruin and desolation.

"In this dilemma what was to be done? The officers held a council, in which it was determined to march one day longer in the direction of Upper Sandusky, and if they should not reach the town in the course of a day, to make a retreat with all possible speed.

"The march was commenced the next morning, through the plains of Sandusky, and continued until two o'clock, when the advance guard was attacked and driven in by the Indians, who were discovered in large numbers in the high grass with which the place was covered. The Indian army was at that moment about entering a large piece of wood almost entirely surrounded by plains; but in this they were disappointed by a rapid movement of the whites. The battle then commenced by a heavy fire from both sides. From a partial possession of the woods, which they had gained at the outset of the battle, the Indians were soon dislodged. They then attempted to gain a small skirt of wood on the right flank of Colonel Crawford, but were prevented from so doing by Major Leet, who at the time commanded the right wing. The firing was heavy and incessant until dark, when it ceased, and both armies lay on their arms during the night.

"In the morning Colonel Crawford's army occupied the battle-ground of the preceding day. The Indians made no attack during the day until late in the evening, but were seen in large bodies traversing the plains in various directions. Some of them appeared to be carrying off the dead and wounded.

"In the morning of this day a council of officers was held, and a retreat was resolved on as the only means of saving the army, the Indians appearing to increase in numbers every hour.

"During the day preparations were made for a retreat by burying the dead, burning fires over the graves to prevent discovery, and preparing means for carrying off the wounded. The retreat was to commence in the course of the night. The Indians, however, became apprised of the intended retreat, and about sundown attacked the army with great force and fury, in every direction except that of Sandusky. When the line of march was formed and the retreat commenced, Colonel Crawford's guides prudently took the direction of Sandusky, which afforded the only opening in the Indian lines and the only chance of concealment. After marching about a mile in this direction the army wheeled about to the left, and by a circuitous route, gained before day the trail by which they came. They continued their march the whole of the next day, without further annoyance than the firing of a few distant shots by the Indians at the rear-guard, which slightly wounded two or three men.

"But several parties, supposing that they could more effectually secure their safety by breaking off from the main army in small numbers, were pursued by the Indians and nearly all of them slain.

"At the commencement of the retreat Colonel Crawford placed himself at the head of the army, and continued there until they had gone about a quarter of a mile, when, missing his son, John Crawford, his son-in-law, Major Harrison, and his nephews, Major Rose and William Crawford, he halted and called for them as the line passed, but without finding them. After the army had passed him he was unable to overtake it, owing to the weariness of his horse. Falling in company with Dr. Knight and two others, they traveled all night, to avoid the pursuit of the Indians.

"On the next day they fell in with Captain John Biggs and Lieutenant Ashley, the latter of whom was wounded. Two others were in company with Biggs and Ashley. They encamped together the succeeding night. On the next day, while on their march, they were attacked by a party of Indians, who made Colonel Crawford and Dr. Knight prisoners.

"'The colonel and I,' says Dr. Knight, 'were then taken to the Indian camp, which was about half a mile from the place where we were captured. On Sunday evening five Delawares, who had posted themselves at some distance further on the road, brought back to the camp where we lay Captain Biggs's and Lieutenant Ashley's scalps, with an Indian scalp which Captain Biggs had taken in the field of action. They also brought in Biggs's horse and mine. They told us the two other men got away from them.

"'Monday morning, the 10th of June, we were paraded to march to Sandusky, about thirty-three miles distant. They had eleven prisoners of us and four scalps, the Indians being seventeen in number.

"'Colonel Crawford was very desirous to see a certain Simon Girty, who lived among the Indians, and was on this account permitted to go to town the same night, with two warriors to guard him, they having orders at the same time to pass by the place where the colonel had turned out his horse, that they might if possible find him. The rest of us were taken as far as the old town (Sandusky), which was within eight miles of the new.

"'Tuesday morning, the 11th, Colonel Crawford was brought out of town on purpose to be marched in with the other prisoners. I asked the colonel if he had seen Mr. Girty. He told me he had, and that Girty had promised to do everything in his power for him, but that the Indians were very much enraged against the prisoners, particularly Captain Pipe, one of the chiefs; he likewise told me that Girty had informed him that his son-in-law, Colonel Harrison, and his nephew, William Crawford, were made prisoners by the Shawnees, but had been pardoned. This Captain Pipe had come from the towns about an hour before Colonel Crawford, and had painted all the prisoners' faces black.

"'As he was painting me, he told me I should go to the Shawnee towns* and see my friends. When the colonel arrived he painted him black also; told him he was glad to see him, and that he would have him shaved when he came to see his friends at the Wyandot town. When we marched, the colonel and I were kept between Pipe and Wingenim, the two Delaware chiefs; the other nine prisoners were sent forward with a party of Indians. As we went along we saw four of the prisoners lying by the path, tomahawked and scalped; some of them were at the distance of half a mile from the others. When we arrived within half a mile of the place where the colonel was executed, we overtook the five prisoners that remained alive. The Indians had caused them to sit down on the ground; also the colonel and myself at some distance from them. I was then given in charge of an Indian fellow to be taken to the Shawnee towns.

"'In the place where we were now made to sit down, there were a number of squaws and boys, who fell on the five prisoners and tomahawked them. There was a certain John McKinley among the prisoners, formerly an officer in the 13th Virginia Regiment, whose head an old squaw cut off. The young Indian fellows came often where the colonel and I were, and dashed the scalps in our faces. We were then conducted along

---

*Pickaway Plains, on the Scioto River.

EARLY SETTLEMENTS.

towards the place where the colonel was afterwards executed. When we came within half a mile of it, Simon Girty met us, with several Indians on horseback. He spoke to the colonel; but as I was about one hundred and fifty yards behind, I could not hear what passed between them.

"'Almost every Indian we met struck us with fist or sticks. Girty waited till I was brought up, and then asked: "Is that the doctor?" I answered, "Yes," and went toward him, reaching out my hand; but he bid me begone, and called me a damned rascal; upon which the fellow who had me in charge pulled me along. Girty rode up after me, and told me that I was to go to the Shawnee towns.

"'When we came to the fire, the colonel was stripped naked, ordered to sit down by the fire, and then they beat him with sticks and fists. Presently after I was treated in the same manner.

"'They then tied a rope to the foot of a post, about fifteen feet high, bound the colonel's hands behind his back, and fastened the rope to the ligature between his wrists. The rope was long enough either for him to sit down or walk round the post once or twice, and return the same way. The colonel then called to Girty, and asked if they intended to burn him? Girty answered, "Yes." The colonel said he would take it all patiently. Upon this Captain Pipe, a Delaware chief, made a speech to the Indians, consisting of about thirty or forty men, and sixty or seventy squaws and boys.

"'When the speech was finished, they all yelled a hideous and hearty assent to what had been said. The Indian men then took up their guns and shot powder into the colonel's body, from his feet as far up as his neck. I think not less than seventy loads were discharged upon his naked body. They then crowded about him, and to the best of my observation, cut off his ears. When the throng had dispersed a little, I saw the blood running from both sides of his head.

"'The fire was about six or seven yards from the post to which the colonel was tied; it was made of small hickory poles, burnt quite through in the middle, each end of the poles remaining about six feet in length. Three or four Indians, by turns, would take up individually one of these burning pieces of wood and apply it to his naked body, already burnt black with powder. These tormentors presented themselves on every side of him, so that whichever way he ran round the post they met him with the burning fagots and poles. Some of the squaws took broad boards, upon which they would put a quantity of burning coals and hot embers and throw them on him, so that in a short time he had nothing but coals of fire and hot ashes to walk upon.

"'In the midst of these extreme tortures, he called to Simon Girty, and begged him to shoot him; but Girty making no answer, he called him again. Girty then, by way of derision, told the colonel he had no gun, and at the same time turning about to an Indian who was behind him, laughed heartily, and by all his gestures seemed delighted at the horrid scene.

"'Girty then came up to me and bade me prepare for death. He said, however, "I was not to die at that place, but to be burnt at the Shawnee towns. He swore by G—d I need not expect to escape death, but should suffer it in all its horrors."

"'Colonel Crawford, at this period of his suffering, besought the Almighty to have mercy on his soul, spoke very low, and bore his torments with the most manly fortitude. He continued, in all the extremities of pain, for an hour and three-quarters or two hours longer, as near as I can judge, when, at last, being almost spent, he lay down on his belly. They then scalped him, and repeatedly threw the scalp in my face, telling me, "That is your great captain's." An old squaw (whose appearance every way answered the idea people entertained of the devil) got a board, and took a parcel of coals and ashes and laid them on his back and head after he had been scalped. He then raised upon his feet and began to walk round the post. They next put a burning stick to him, but he seemed more insensible to pain than before. After he expired, his body was thrown into the fire and consumed to ashes.'"

One of the earliest settlers was David Morgan, a man of great energy of character and sterling worth. He was a near relative of General Morgan, of Revolutionary memory.

"At the time we speak of, Mr. Morgan was living near Prickett's Fort, about twelve miles above Morgantown and close to the Monongahela River. He was then sixty years of age, and for some days had been slightly indisposed. Early in April, 1779, he desired two of his children, Stephen, sixteen years of age, and Sarah, about fourteen, to feed the stock at his farm, distant about one mile on the opposite side of the river. This he did in consequence of feeling worse that morning than usual. No Indians had yet been seen in the neighborhood, and, of course, he considered all perfectly safe. As the weather was fine, the brother and sister concluded to remain and prepare a piece of ground for melons. Soon after they left the fort—for they were then at the stockade—Mr. Morgan lay down, and shortly falling to sleep dreamed that he saw the children walking before him *scalped*. This vision awoke him, and finding upon inquiry that the children had not returned, he became uneasy and started immediately in hunt of them. Approaching the premises, he beheld his children busily engaged in the manner already indicated.

"Seating himself upon a log close at hand, Morgan watched his children for some time, when suddenly he saw emerge from the house two Indians, who moved rapidly up toward Stephen and his sister. Fearing to alarm the children, Morgan cautiously warned them of their danger and told them to go at once to the fort. They instantly obeyed, and the Indians, discovering their movements, gave their accustomed whoop and started in pursuit. Morgan, having hitherto escaped their attention, now arose, and returning their shout caused the savages to seek behind trees instant protection.

"Knowing that the chances for a fair fight were almost hopeless, Morgan thought to escape by running, and so manage as to keep the trees between himself and the enemy. In this, however, he was mistaken. Impaired health and the infirmities of age disabled him from keeping long beyond the reach of the fleet and athletic warriors. Finding, after a run of some two hundred yards, that the savages were rapidly gaining on him, he determined to shoot one and take his chances with the other. Turning to fire, both Indians sprang behind trees, and Morgan did the same; but finding the tree he first gained too small to protect his person, he quitted it and made for another, which was reached in safety.

"One of the Indians, hoping to get nearer his intended victim, ran to the tree which Morgan had left, but finding it too small, threw himself behind a log close at hand. This, however, did not conceal him entirely, which Morgan noticing, instantly fired, and shot the savage through the part exposed. Feeling himself mortally wounded, with more than Spartan fortitude the Indian drew his knife and inflicted two deep stabs upon his breast. To him death had no terrors, save as dealt by the hand of his white antagonist.

"The heroic old man having thus effectually disposed of one of his pursuers, again resorted to flight. The chances were now desperate, as the Indian had the double advantage of tomahawk and rifle. Running fifty or sixty yards, he glanced hurriedly over his shoulder just in time to see the savage ready to fire. Jumping to one side, the ball passed harmlessly by, and the two felt that the combat must be brought to close quarters. With all the fury of his nature the savage rushed upon his adversary with loud yells and uplifted tomahawk. Morgan prepared to meet him with his gun, but the savage aimed a blow with his tomahawk with such force and effect as to knock the rifle from Morgan's grasp, and cut two of the fingers from his left hand. They now clinched, and the combat became equal, except the savage was the younger and much more powerful of the two. Frantic at the loss of his companion and his own ill success, he fought with a desperation rarely known in a single combat. Morgan, on the other part, inspirited by the success which had thus far attended him, nerved his arm and strung every muscle to the conflict, resolved to kill his combatant or sell his life as dearly as possible. Our hero in his younger days had been a most expert wrestler, and was thus enabled with ease to throw the Indian; but the latter, more active and powerful, readily turned him. With a yell of exultation the savage now held his adversary down and began to feel for his knife. Morgan saw the movement, and well knew all would be over if the savage got possession of it.

"The Indian was prevented getting the knife by a woman's apron, which he had wrapped around his body in such a manner as to confine the handle. Whilst endeavoring to extricate it Morgan got one of the Indian's thumbs between his teeth, and so effectually ground it that the poor wretch was sadly disconcerted, and more than once screamed with pain. Finally he grasped his knife, but so close to the blade that Morgan, noticing it, caught the end of the handle and drew it through the Indian's hand, cutting it severely. The savage was now literally *hors de combat*, and, springing to his feet, endeavored to get away; but the resolute Morgan, not yet having done with him, held on to the thumb until he had inflicted a mortal thrust in the side of the enemy. Letting go, the Indian sank almost lifeless to the ground, and Morgan made his way to the fort."

Captain Samuel Brady resided at one time in Wellsburg. He was tall, rather slender, and very active. He usually wore instead of a hat, a black handkerchief around his head. From his peculiar appearance, he was well known to the Indians.

"A party of Indians having made an inroad into the Sewickley settlement, committing barbarous murders and carrying off some prisoners, Brady set off in pursuit with only five men and his *pet* Indian. He came up with them, and discovered that they were encamped on the banks of the Mahoning. Having reconnoitered their position, Brady posted his men, and in the deepest silence awaited the break of day, when the Indians arose and stood around their fires. At a given signal seven rifles cracked, and five Indians were dead. The remaining Indians instantly disappeared.

"Brady being out with his party on one occasion, had reached Slippery Rock Creek, a branch of the Beaver, without seeing signs of Indians. Here, however, he came on an Indian trail in the evening, which he followed till dark, without overtaking the Indians. The next morning he renewed his pursuit, and overtook them while they were engaged at their morning meal. Unfortunately for him another party of Indians were in his rear. They had fallen upon his trail and pursued him, doubtless with as much ardor as had characterized his own pursuit. At the moment he fired upon the Indians in his front, he was in turn fired upon by those in his rear. He was now between two fires, and vastly outnumbered. Two of his men fell, his tomahawk was shot from his side, and the battle yell was given by the party in his rear, and loudly returned and repeated by those in his front. There was no time for hesitation, no safety in delay, no chance for successful defense in their present position. Brady ran towards the creek. He was known by many, if not by all of them; and there were the scores to be settled between him and them. They knew the country well; he did not, and from his running towards the creek they were certain of taking him prisoner. The creek was, for a long distance above and below the point he was approaching, washed in its channel to a great depth. In the certain expectation of catching him there, the private soldiers of his party were disregarded; and throwing down their guns and drawing their tomahawks, all pressed forward to seize their victim. Quick of eye, fearless of heart, and determined never to be a captive to the Indians, Brady comprehended their object and his only chance for escape the moment he saw the creek; and by one mighty effort of courage and activity, defeated the one and effected the other. He sprang across the abyss of waters, and stood rifle in hand on the opposite bank in safety. As quick as lightning his rifle was primed, for it was his invariable practice in loading, to prime first. The next minute the powder-horn was at the gun's muzzle; when, as he was in this act, a large Indian, who had been foremost in the pursuit, came to the opposite bank, and with the manliness of a generous foe who scorns to undervalue the qualities of an enemy, said, in a loud voice and tolerable English: 'Blady make good jump.'

"His leap was about twenty-three feet, and the water was twenty feet deep. Brady's next effort was to gather up his men. They immediately commenced their homeward march, and returned to Pittsburg about half defeated. Three Indians had been seen to fall from the fire they gave them at breakfast."

Another famous border hero was Lewis Wetzel, the son of John Wetzel, a German, who settled on Big Wheeling Creek, about fourteen miles from the Ohio River, and was killed by the Indians in 1777, when Lewis was about twenty-three years of age. The education of Lewis, like most of his contemporaries, was that of the hunter and warrior. When a boy, he adopted the practice of loading and firing his rifle as he ran. On account of his father's death, he and his brothers, of whom he had five, vowed sleepless vengeance against the whole Indian race.

"During the life-time of his father, when he was about thirteen years of age, Lewis was taken prisoner by the Indians, together with his brother Jacob, about eleven years old. Before he was taken he received a slight wound in the breast from a bullet, which carried off a small piece of his breast-bone. The second night after they were taken, the Indians encamped at Big Lick, twenty miles from the river, on the waters of McMechen's Creek. The boys were not confined. After the Indians had fallen asleep, Lewis whispered to his brother Jacob that he must get up and go back home with him. Jacob at first objected, but afterwards got up and went along with him. When they had gone about one hundred

EARLY SETTLEMENTS.

yards from the camp, they sat down on a log. 'Well,' said Lewis, 'we can not go home barefooted; I will go back and get a pair of moccasins for each of us,' and accordingly did so, and returned. After sitting a little longer, 'Now,' said he, 'I will go back and get father's gun, and then we will start.' This he effected. They had not traveled far on the trail by which they came before they heard the Indians coming after them. It was a moonlight night. When the Indians came pretty near them, they stepped aside into the bushes, let them pass, then fell into the rear and traveled on. The next day they reached Wheeling in safety, crossing from the Indian shore to Wheeling Island on a raft of their own making. By this time Lewis had been almost spent from his wound.

"Belmont County, Ohio, was the scene of several of the most daring adventures of this far-famed borderer. Once while hunting, Wetzel fell in with a young man who lived on Dunkard Creek, and was persuaded to accompany him to his home. On their arrival they found the house in ruins and all the family murdered, except a young woman who had been bred with them, and to whom the young man was ardently attached. She was taken alive, as was found by examining the trail of the enemy, who were three Indians and a white renegade. Burning with revenge, they followed the trail, until opposite the mouth of Captina, where the enemy had crossed. They swam the stream, and discovered the Indian camp, around the fires of which lay the enemy in careless repose. The young woman was apparently unhurt, but was making much moaning and lamentation. The young man, hardly able to restrain his rage, was for firing and rushing instantly upon them. Wetzel, more cautious, told him to wait until daylight, when there would be a better chance of success in killing the whole party. After dawn the Indians prepared to depart. The young man selecting the white renegade, and Wetzel the Indian, they both fired simultaneously, with fatal effect. The young man rushed forward, knife in hand, to relieve the mistress of his affections, while Wetzel reloaded and pursued the two surviving Indians, who had taken to the woods until they could ascertain the number of their enemies. Wetzel, as soon as he was discovered, discharged his rifle at random, in order to draw them from their covert. The ruse took effect, and taking to his heels, he loaded as he ran, and suddenly wheeling about, discharged his rifle through the body of his nearest and unsuspecting enemy. The remaining Indian, seeing the fate of his companion, and that his enemy's gun was unloaded, rushed forward with all energy, the prospect of prompt revenge being fairly before him. Wetzel led him on, dodging from tree to tree, until his rifle was again ready, when suddenly turning, he fired, and his remaining enemy fell dead at his feet. After taking their scalps, Wetzel and his friend, with their rescued captive, returned in safety to the settlement.

"In the year 1782, after Crawford's defeat, Lewis went with a Thomas Mills, who had been in the campaign, to get his horse, which he had left near the place where St. Clairsville now stands. At the Indian springs, two miles from St. Clairsville, on the Wheeling road, they were met by about forty Indians, who were in pursuit of the stragglers from the campaign. The Indians and the white men discovered each other about the same moment. Lewis fired first and killed an Indian, while the Indians wounded Mills in the heel, who was soon overtaken and killed. Four of the Indians then singled out, dropped their guns, and pursued Wetzel. Wetzel loaded his rifle as he ran. After running about half a mile, one of the Indians having gotten within eight or ten steps of him, Wetzel wheeled round and shot him down, ran and loaded his gun as before. After running about three-quarters of a mile further, a second Indian came so close to him that, when he turned to fire, the Indian caught the muzzle of his gun, and, as he expressed it, 'he and the Indian had a severe wring.' He, however, succeeded in bringing the muzzle to the Indian's breast, and killed him on the spot. By this time he, as well as the Indian, was pretty well tired out; yet the pursuit was continued by the two remaining Indians. Wetzel, as before, loaded his gun and stopped several times during this latter chase; when he did so the Indians treed themselves. After going something more than a mile, Wetzel took advantage of a little open piece of ground over which the Indians were passing, a short distance behind him, to make a sudden stop for the purpose of shooting the foremost, who got behind a little sapling which was too small to cover his body. Wetzel shot and broke his thigh. The wound, in the issue, proved fatal. The last of the Indians then gave a little yell, and said, 'No catch that man, gun always loaded,' and gave up the chase, glad, no doubt, to get off with his life."

In 1779 Stephen Collins, of Halifax County, Virginia, "long hunter of deer-skins," who had for years followed his uncertain calling in the wild region west of the Blue Ridge, with five of his brothers (only one unmarried) and a brother-in-law, removed to

"A MOUNTAIN TARN."

Kentucky. The writer has often heard his son (Judge Joel Collins, of Oxford, Ohio), tell the story of the transit over the mountains.* Two feather-beds, securely and tightly rolled, were slung on a horse and so arranged, one on each side, that the larger children could climb on to the secure perch when weary or footsore from the long march. The gentlest horses had pack-saddles made of two large split hampers, in each of which two children fitted. The pack-horses of rougher tempers carried corn-meal, bacon, salt, camp furniture, and the clothing of the entire party. In addition there was a horse for each woman. The five families had over twenty horses and some fifty head of cattle. The baggage-train was packed for the day's march while the women dressed the children and cooked the breakfast. The cattle were driven in the van, and the long train of horses came on in single file, two of the men walking behind to rearrange breaks and pick up any mischievous urchin who managed to slip out of the hampers. The party of brothers first settled at Bowman's Station, on Dick's Creek, which they reached "in fairly good condition, although for most of the journey they had no meat except such game as the hunters could find, and to find any they had sometimes to make long excursions away from the rough trail upon which the cattle and horses must be kept." From the time of their arrival in Kentucky they "dressed in deer-skins, made their beds of buffalo-skins stretched on rough wood frames, with the woolly side up, and had for covering

---

* The stalwart figure and genial, kindly face of the "Old Judge" will be remembered by every student of Miami University, where, for so many years, he was custodian of the buildings and superintendent of the grounds and lands In his youth a good soldier and a daring scout, from his sixteenth year he was in every battle where the collected force of Kentucky fought the Indians. He lived through the "hard times" of the West, a rough, rugged life of want and self-denial; but the metal in the man was so fine that he had brought through it a character fashioned for all noble uses upon the anvil of adversity.

a second buffalo-skin with the wool turned down." Their shirts were made from a species of nettle which were beaten to a lint that could be spun into yarn.

Indians were constantly prowling about the station, and occasionally a messenger or a hunter was shot and scalped near the fort. The Collins families had not been long in Kentucky before the brothers were called out with the militia, under General George Rogers Clark, to "make a raid into the Indian country on the north of the Ohio, and put down with the strong hand the skulking varmints who were murdering peaceable settlers." The *special provocation* was the capture of Alexander McConnell, an express-rider from Lexington.

"The Indians shot his horse under him, tied his hands behind him, and drove him at a run to their hiding-place on the Licking. A scouting party from the station found the dead horse, and so we knew he was a prisoner. I was only a little fellow about eight years old, but I remember yet the rumpus at the station the week after his capture, when some of our men, who were in the field near by, saw a wretched object, with a few rags around him, coming towards them. They halted him with their rifles up at sight, when he called out, 'I am Alec McConnell.' I never can forget how the women and we youngsters run, and how we crowded around after he had something to eat, to hear his story. He had been with them three days when he got away. That third night, when the Indians were sleeping, he managed to slip his hands out of the thongs (he had mighty small hands), then he untied his legs from the stakes to which they were fastened, and got hold of the Indians' guns. One by one he pulled them over to him. He put one gun on each knee, with the muzzles almost touching the heads of the two nearest to him; then, as soon as he fired, he snatched up the loaded rifles one by one, and killed three more. He thought he marked some of the skunks that got away; but they run so fast he was n't sure, and he had no time to lose looking, as they were all on the other side of the Ohio. He had to do his best to get over to this side before daylight. He picked out a splendid tomahawk and the best rifle, broke the locks of the others, and got back to the station without meeting either Indian or white man."

EARLY SETTLEMENTS. 93

In 1780, when General George Rogers Clark called out the militia for a "defensive raid to the Indian villages," Stephen Collins and his brothers went with the Lexington company. Clark's command consisted of two regiments. One, commanded by Colonel Ben Logan, assembled at Bryant's Spring, eight miles from Lexington, and marched down the Licking to its mouth; the other, commanded by Colonel Wm. Linn, marched from the falls, up the Ohio to the Licking. The transportation of artillery, provisions, and military stores was in skiffs, under charge of Colonel George Slaughter, with one hundred and fifty troops, raised in Virginia. The entire force consisted of one thousand men. They crossed the Ohio, 2d of August, 1780, and marched to the Indian towns with a six-pound howitzer, for which a way through the forest had to be opened. On the 6th they reached Chillicothe, on the Little Miami. The Indian town was abandoned, and still burning. They arrived at Piqua, on the north bank of Mad River, on the 8th; had a severe fight with the Indians; took the town, burnt it, and destroyed the growing corn. As Judge Collins told the story, Clark avoided an ambuscade by returning across the country by a different route, to their point of departure at the Licking. Soon after the Collins's return they moved to Lexington.

Joel Collins's first school-master was John McKinney, better known in Kentucky as "Wildcat McKinney." He had been disabled in the fight at Point Pleasant, in 1774, where he was one of the Virginia riflemen. He was shot through both thighs, and fell. His party were driven a short distance, and he was left lying about half-way between the combatants, who fought Indian fashion, from the cover of a tree. McKinney made an effort to crawl back to the riflemen, when he was seen by an

Indian, and another shot shattered his left arm so badly that the splintered bone stuck in the bark of a paw-paw bush to which he was holding. The Indians made a rush with their tomahawks, but the Virginians came to his relief. Beating back the Indians, they carried him off safely. In the last part of this hand-to-hand fray he had two ribs broken by the stroke of a tomahawk. Thinking his fighting days were over, he took up the occupation of a school-master and came out to Kentucky. One morning in June the women of the station were up very early milking the cows, when Mrs. Collins called to her husband:

"Stephen! Stephen! run over to the school-house; something's the matter with the master."

Mr. Collins, with Joel at his heels, ran over without loss of time. The door was open, and Collins asked: "What's the matter?" McKinney sung out: "It's an ugly baste tryin' to kill me; but I've got him purty well whipped." And he went on plugging away with his lame left hand into the side of an animal which he held doubled up in his right arm, and pressed against the table, although its teeth were clinched in his breast a little below his throat. Mr. Collins did his best to help him, but he insisted: "Wait until I get to the door, so you can see how to take the pesky thing's teeth out of me breast-bone." It took all Mr. Collins's knowledge of surgery to free the school-master. "Wildcat McKinney" moved from Kentucky to Missouri in 1820.

Young Joel Collins began his career as an Indian fighter in 1791, in the expedition to the Indian towns on the Wabash. This gave him "a liking for the army," and he enlisted in the "pack-horse brigade," which was constantly on the march, taking supplies to the advanced posts on the Miami. He was at

EARLY SETTLEMENTS. 95

Fort Hamilton when Little Turtle and his warriors struck the war-pole, and took the trail for Columbia. On their return they made a night attack on the "pack-horse brigade" encampment. There was severe and close fighting until daylight, when the guns from the fort were effective, and the Indians retreated. During the fight one of his comrades was badly wounded, and he would have been tomahawked and scalped had not Joel Collins brought him on his back to the shelter of the fort. To use the vernacular of the time, "he was a born soldier." Like the war-horse, "he smelleth the battle from afar," and the writer has often heard him say that "the deepest regret of his life was that he had not fought in the Revolution under Washington," a natural regret when one understands the times in which he lived. For although the Western pioneers were out of the way of the fight when the Revolution began, for them to stay out of the fray was wholly impossible. The blood of the men who fought at Derry was in their veins; and that blood never ran slowly or grew cold when burning powder scented the air. They were hundreds of miles away from the sea-board; but here and there a solitary hunter crossed the mountain-chain alone to join the rebels under Washington; or little groups of two or three fell together by the way, and marched steadily over the ridges and through the winding ravines, until, from the Blue Mountain Heights, they looked down upon the very center of the Old Dominion, that fair county of Albemarle, which was the birth-place of the most resolute soldier and daring leader who ever headed a foray into the Indian country.

"When the Independence of the Colonies was secured, but few of these frontiersmen had won through the battles and the winter at Valley Forge. None of the survivors were above want. This poverty of the soldiers was imposed by circumstances. The times were in fault. Continental money was worthless. Six years of service left them nothing. Maimed, ragged, and foot-sore, men returned to the little farms, where the outlying fields were wastes, and only the patches of corn around the cabins told the story of how brave women had fought the battle of life for their children during the long years of self-dependence. To quote from a trustworthy historian of the time:

"If want of provisions or other causes made a visit to a neighbour's necessary, a settler's wife must either take her children with her through the woods, or leave them unprotected, under the most fearful apprehension that some mischief might befall them before her return. As bread and meat were scarce, milk was the principal dependence for the support of the family. One cow of each family was provided with a bell, which could be heard from half a mile to a mile, and in the mornings the mother placed herself in the most favorable position for listening to her cow-bell, which she knew as well as she did the voice of her child. She could detect her own even among a clamour of many other bells, thus manifesting a nicety of ear which, with cultivation, might have been envied by the best musicians.

"If her children were small, she tied them in bed to prevent them from wandering, and to guard them from danger from fire and snakes; then, guided by the tinkling of the bell, made her way through the tall meads, and across the ravines, until she found the object of her search; happy on her return to find her children unharmed."

To glance for a moment at the position of the River Clearings, we find that the settlements of the Scotch-Irish from Bedford, York Pennsylvania, and Virginia, with a few families directly from the North of Ireland, soon extended from the Monongahela to the Ohio. Their route was the barely practicable road called Braddock's trail.

Uncertain of the boundaries of Virginia and Pennsylvania,

few applied for land-warrants, although Lord Dunmore had opened offices for the granting of warrants within the bounds of what are now the four western counties of Pennsylvania. They were, however, afterwards recognized as actual settlers, and thus entitled to farms not exceeding four hundred acres.

At the close of *Pontiac's War*, in the fall of 1763-64, the stream of emigration was greatly enlarged. In the *Historical Sketches of Western Presbyterianism*, the author says:

"It was a remarkable circumstance that between Mr. Smith's congregations and the Ohio, and along up and down the river for thirty or forty miles below Pittsburg, there was early settled, or 'squatted' rather, a peculiar population, many of them from Eastern Virginia, *well-suited from their habits and training as hunters, and from their adoption of the Indian modes of warfare, to fight with the savages, and to act as a life-guard, as a protecting cordon, to Mr. Smith's people, and to the interior settlements.*

In counting them up by families, he mentions in the *Life Guard*, "the *Bradys*, the *Wetzels*, and the *Poes*," then he goes on telling of "a glorious work of grace began and long continued in that vineyard which God had so strangely fenced around." He again singles out for special mention "Mr. Smith," whose "dress was always neat and becoming. His voice was remarkable alike for the *terrific* and the *pathetic* (the italics are preserved not inserted), and as Dr. Kirkland said of the celebrated Fisher Ames, 'now like the thunder, and now like the music of heaven,'" then he continues: "I never heard a man who could so completely unbar the gates of hell, and make me look so far down into the dark, bottomless abyss." The historian, after further characterizing his pulpit hero as one who left "the cold ratiocinations of logic far behind," grows facetiously comparative, and tells us of "old Colonel R—, of Virginia, who "used to say that he liked that preacher best who could make him wish that he could creep into an augur-hole before the preacher was done," and he clinches this with another indorsement: "Robert Morris, the great financier, who saved the credit of his country and ruined his own, once told Dr. Rush that he 'liked that kind of preaching that drives a man into the corner of his pew, and makes him think the devil is after him.' *He* would have been delighted with Mr. Smith." That we may have an opportunity to prove the authenticity of his anecdotal lore, he naively refers us to *Hazard's Register*, Vol. XII, page 249.

To give these fiery sectarists their due, they were a bold, hardy, simple-minded people; ready and willing to toil in the fields with their rifles within reach, and equally ready to listen "to the preaching of the Word" with the same rifles in their hands. One more story of their struggle with want and we will see that there was a full-hearted generosity in the composition of these Irish "seceders," who are immortalized by Virginia's sweetest and truest poet, in three lines:—

> "Upon their dinted shields, no crests;
> No glittering orders on their breasts,
> But iron in their blood."

Mr. Smith had found a spiritual and faithful people, but they were too poor to pay a salary which would support his family. He, in common with all, must cultivate a farm. He bought one on the security of the salary pledged by his congregation.

Year after year went by with the salary unpaid. The last payment was due, and neither the preacher nor the elders could pay it. The case was laid before the people. Mr. Moore, who owned the only mill in the country, offered to grind their wheat (which was their currency), on the most reasonable terms.

EARLY SETTLEMENTS.

Wheat was abundant, but it could not be sold for more than twelve and a half cents per bushel, in cash; and they were compelled to bring salt across the mountains at an exchange of twenty-one bushels of wheat for one of salt. The people gave generously of their grain, although some had to bring it from sixteen to twenty-six miles to the mill. In a month the flour was ready to go to market. After the service was over on Sunday (the only day in the week on which all the people were gathered together), the question was asked: "Who will run the flour to New Orleans?" It was a perilous and daring venture. Many a boat's crew had gone down the river without even one of them returning to tell where the others had perished. The young men were silent, and the middle-aged stammered excuses, which all who shrunk from the undertaking must accept. At length one of the elders, tall, brawny, and white-haired, his face marked with the toil of nearly seventy years arose and said simply: "Here am I; send me." Pastor and people united in remonstrance, but the old man was firm. To keep their pastor and release his home from debt he was ready to brave danger and face death. Two young men were induced to go with him, and pastor and people together marched fifteen miles to the river to say "Godspeed" to the brave elder. A prayer was made, a hymn was sung, and the old Scotchman called out: "Untie the cable, and let us see what the Lord will do for us." Nearly ten months had passed without a word from Elder Smiley, when at last a Sunday came when the people found Father Smiley in his accustomed seat. After the services the people were told to come early in the week to hear the report from the sales. Monday the house was full, and after thanks had been given to God, the old man rose and told the story of his mission. He had sold his flour for twenty-seven dollars a barrel, and poured upon the table the largest pile of gold ever seen in the county.

The young men were paid a hundred dollars apiece, and Father Smiley was asked his charges. "He thought," he said, "that he ought to have the same sum as each of the others;" but modestly added, "he had not worked as hard." When the money was counted there was enough to pay Mr. Smith's entire dues, to advance the sum of his next year's salary, give Father Smiley three hundred dollars, and then pay a dividend to each contributor of wheat.

Up to 1793 the frontier was a constant scene of hand-to-hand fights and Indian inroads. Gradually the savages had been driven back, until the Ohio River was the battle-line, across which, however, a daring chief would occasionally lead a wild raid through the wilderness tracts between the sparse settlements; or a solitary warrior would come on a "still hunt" for scalps, and lurk in the wooded thickets, until some careless borderer, who had built his lonely cabin in the forest depths, away from the protecting block-house, gave the chance for which he was waiting.

The Indians loved "The White Shining River," and the tribes that had been driven from its neighborhood retreated to the upper waters of the Scioto and the Miamis, that the warriors might be free to renew the contest for its possession without the encumbrance of villages to protect; and so, day after day, somewhere on "The Beautiful River," a battle was fought, or a fatal bullet or whizzing tomahawk struck the invader of the hunting-grounds. In the cool, green recesses of the woods, a stealthy foe would sometimes stalk the frontiersman, who, in eager pursuit of a startled deer, forgot to be watchful, forgot that he himself was game to be hunted. Yet, even then, the odds were not altogether against the frontiersman, if, in the profound stillness, when he stopped to sight the game, a sudden snap of twig or bough, or even so small a thing as the fluttering rustle of a broken leaf, told the acute and listening senses of a danger to be averted or confronted. Even then, so ready was he in the game, so determined to triumph through some wily device, some trick of skill he had learned from the foe, some twist or turn of the hunter's or woodman's art, that—being warned—the *odds* were *even*. If it was too late for skill, it was never too late for daring. If the rifle snapped, or the flint failed, he would turn on his antagonist and face him as calmly as if he were proof against attack, knowing that a duel, without help or witness, had begun, and that one of the duelists would never leave the fateful glade.

The frontiersmen went down in many a hand-to-hand fight; yet despite their losses, they were in time the owners of Kentucky, and lords paramount of the river. They were men of determination as well as courage, accustomed to hardship, skilled in all the strategy of the border. They overmatched the Indian in bodily strength, and with his own weapons foiled him in the game of war.

They were a product of race, tempered by the exigencies of a life which was forced to win its innings under the constant pressure of danger. With a certain show of justice, they insisted that their raids upon the Indian villages were raids of reprisal, for in the lexicon of the frontier a war of defense meant a war of extermination.

In their leather-belted hunting-shirts, furnished with sockets for tomahawk, knife, and pistol, with bullet-pouch, powder-horn, and hunting cup, thrown across a brawny chest, and carrying with ease and a certain careless grace a heavy rifle, the frontiersmen were picturesque and stalwart figures, admirably in keeping with the wild background of vine-shrouded trees and dim forest aisles in which history and fancy has framed them. They belonged to the dense woodland solitudes, to the tangled wilderness, through which the wandering brooks and the shaded creeks found their way to "The Shining River."

CHAPTER V.

INDIAN CONFLICTS ON AND FOR THE RIVER.

WOLFE'S victory at Quebec, September the 4th, 1756, virtually won Canada for the English, although the actual surrender of the New France dates at Montreal, September the 8th, 1760.

Immediately after the surrender, Major Robert Rogers was sent to take formal possession of the forts upon the lakes included in the capitulation of Montreal. Before reaching Detroit the astute officer clearly understood that there was a dangerous enemy to placate, an offended and resistant power to conciliate, before the English could reap any of the fruitful results of victory.

On the south-west shore of Lake Erie, the present site of Cleveland, Pontiac met the expedition. The opening speech of the Great Chief threatened a stormy ending; yet Rogers's thorough understanding of Indian character and Indian diplomacy secured for the English troops an unmolested passage to Detroit. The surrender of the fort was demanded, the lilies of France were lowered from the flag-staff, and the cross of St. George was uplifted over the Key to the Western Lakes.

Neither the population of the town of Detroit, which, according to Rogers's estimate, amounted to about twenty-five hundred inhabitants, nor the Indian allies of the French living in numerous villages around and near the fort, offered any opposition to the change of rulers, except the opposition suggested in Pontiac's proud definition of the terms of settlement, and the significant warning that he would "drive out the English and shut up the door" if the terms which he had accepted at the council were violated.

In the interval between the capitulation of Montreal and the treaty of Paris (February 10, 1763), which finally adjusted some minor difficulties in the terms of peace, the Indians were ill at ease and restless. There were constant rumours of uprisings upon the frontiers. The strong hold the French still had in the North-west was shown in the grand council at Pontiac's village that spring, when all the lake tribes were represented. That Pontiac believed in the final success of the French is beyond question, as is also the fact that the chiefs of the Algonquin Confederacy accepted Pontiac's belief as an immediate reason for war.

To have a clear understanding of the complications upon the border, it is necessary to understand something of the situation of the Indian tribes; and also the ties and the motives that influenced their alliances with the French, with the English, and with each other.

The Indians upon the Illinois, where LA SALLE had planted his colonies, were bound to the colonists by ties of blood, as well as of affection. Soldiers in the forts, traders in the Indian villages, *couriers des bois*, who made their long and often solitary voyages through the lakes and rivers of the North-west, had taken their wives from among the tribes of the Illinois. These Indians were nominally Catholics, therefore the Church sanctioned their marriages. In religion, language, and affection their descendants were French. Thus it very naturally came about that even the most timid—those who, from motives of gain or policy, wished to preserve a strict neutrality between the disaffected chiefs and their new rulers, the English—would not have betrayed the conspiracy of Pontiac if they had been trusted with full knowledge of his plans. Nor was this affiliation of the Illinois with the French an exceptional episode in the history of the lake tribes. It is true that LA SALLE had a wonderful influence over the Indians with whom he was thrown in contact; and, doubtless, he did more than any one man has ever done to impress the savages with respect and admiration for the French character.* Yet it is no less true that from the advent of Champlain, to the death of Montcalm, the French leaders were the models, as they were the admiration, of the greatest of the Indian chieftains.

The governors-of "New France" had made friends of the Western chiefs; and the French soldiers had heartily fraternized with their brave allies. The careless daring, the chivalry, the gayety, all those pronounced characteristics that brighten the camp and gild war, appealed at once to the pride, the imagination, and the fealty of the savage warriors. The sentiment underlying the comradeship so frankly offered captivated fancies that had been fed upon the barbaric traditions of a brave, proud

---

*A story told by the Abbe Renaudot, in his "Relations," illustrates this sympathetic admiration of the Indians for the French: "A New York Hollander said to an Indian 'that the French were the slaves of their king; but that every Hollander was one of the masters in Holland.' 'If that is so,' replied the Indian, 'the slaves are of more value than the masters.'"

race. Their French comrades called them brothers, and treated them as brothers. The French king was their father. The splendour of his glory was reflected upon his children; and the child-like savage did not stint the measure of his admiration or his devotion. When Canada was lost to the French, there was the bitterness of sorrow, as well as of defeat, in the hearts of the Indians. This feeling runs through every sentence of Pontiac's reply to the address of the English officer sent to take possession of the forts. The first few sentences define the situation:

"Englishmen, you know the French king is our father. He promised to be such, and we, in return, promised to be his children. This promise we have kept. Englishmen, you have made war upon our father. You are his enemies. How can you have the boldness to venture here among his children? Do you not know that his enemies are ours? He is old, infirm—he has been sleeping. You have taken advantage of that to possess yourselves of Canada. But he will awaken. I hear him stirring now. He is asking for his Indian children. When he is fully awake he will destroy you utterly."

Any close study of the history of the North American Indian will force upon the unprejudiced student the irresistible conviction that the only race that has ever understood the Indian or treated him fairly was the French. Of all the peoples with whom the North American savage has been thrown in contact, the French alone never contemned or undervalued him. In some degree this is the outcome of a sympathetic and subtle similarity of traits. A likeness that is elusive and indistinct, but which is constantly brought out in the shading of individual character.

The Indian, like the Gascon, vaunts his prowess, and, like the

Gascon, he recklessly faces death to make that vaunt of challenge good. In both races there is the same desperate courage in assault; if fed with hope, the same endurance; if defeated, the same despairing. hopelessness. Alike, they are easily stung to fierce effort by pride of race or devotion to a great leader. They will dare or die like heroes in the first onset of battle; yet if their collected ranks recoil, if their assault fails, they are easily thrown into wild confusion, and their defeat is soon assured.

The surrender of Canada to the English threw the tribes that were allied with the French into "the confusion of defeat." Unhappily for the security of the frontier, the English and the frontiersmen treated them with the scant ceremony which the Indian always resents. The English officers, regarding them as savages, treated them with careless contempt, as though they were the useless portion of the spoil of their recent conquest. Not knowing, or caring to know, any avenue to their favor, they took no pains to find one; not reckoning their value as allies, they provoked their hatred. Soldiers and traders alike were brutal. The French traders were ordered away from the stations upon the slightest pretexts; and the English, who succeeded them, clinched their bargains with the strong hand. Delinquent debtors were treated to blows if the promised furs were not forthcoming at the appointed date; others who brought their peltries were made drunk, cheated, and then kicked out of the trading-house. The resentment of the Indian was deferred; but, with the savage, an indignity suffered is a hate recorded.

When, in addition to their personal wrongs, the public wrong to the tribes, in the conditions which defined the boundaries of the country surrendered by the French at the Treaty of Paris, was added to the general count of grievances, when the Indians learned that all the lands east of the Mississippi, and as far south as the southern boundary of Georgia (the ownership of which had been vested in the Indian Confederacies of the West from time immemorial) was, by the Treaty of Paris, ceded to the English, their rage equaled their hate. The warring confederacies were now ready to make peace with each other, that they might make common cause against the English. Owing to the influence of Sir William Johnson with the Iroquois, the five original tribes of the Six Nations were allies of the English. These tribes, settled in Western New York and North-western Pennsylvania, had resisted the settlement of the "New France" on the upper bank of the St. Lawrence; and they still held bitter memories of successive wars with the French, in which they had sustained disastrous defeats. But with the Algonquin Confederacy of the lake tribes and the Mobilian Confederacy of the South there were no reasons either of policy or friendship for their alliance with, or submission to, the English.

With Pontiac at the head of the Algonquin chiefs, with the smoldering fire of the Cherokee war—which had been kindled by the aggressive spirit of the frontiersmen, who regarded the Indian as a wild beast that must be killed to clear the path—not yet extinguished, there was but little hope of peace or quiet upon the border. The Southern warriors were grimly waiting an opportunity to pay their newly made score; and it was with jealous eyes, clouded by the rankling soreness of defeat, that they watched the movements of the new neighbours defeat had forced upon their acceptance.

Everywhere traders and settlers were pushing their way into the newly acquired territory. Posts and block-houses were being builded upon the banks of the south-eastern tributaries of the

Ohio—west of the route known to the tribes as the "Warrior's Road."*

"THE DARK AND BLOODY GROUND," which, by a tacit understanding between the Northern and Southern Indians, had been reserved from habitation, and held as the wide-spread battle-field of the Nations; the dueling-ground, where wrongs were to be avenged and disputes settled; the place where the shock of war must be met, to protect the far distant villages, and which—when the tribes were at peace—was the free hunting-ground for all, was now beginning to be dotted by long lines of well-laden pack-horses, the advance guard of emigrants coming to settle upon the lands that had been held, from the earliest period to which their traditions dated back, as the common property of the Nations.

In utter disregard of Bouquet's proclamation from Fort Pitt, in 1772, which said: "The treaty of Easton, in 1758, secured to the Indians all lands west of the mountains for their hunting-grounds; wherefore I forbid any, and all, settlements from being made there"—the settlements were made. In the quaint statement of a Western writer: "The savages knew with whom they had to deal; they knew that every white man's fingers itched for the furs and the lands of the Indian; they had learned that each

---

*The Indian confederacies were subdivided into tribes, with their villages and bands of warriors; and also into distinct clans or families, who wore a device or emblem, known in the Algonquin language as *Totems*. Although branches of the different clans might belong to tribes speaking a different language and living in far distant villages, the tie of fraternity was always recognized. Each warrior was as proud of his Totem as any one of the warlike barons was of "The blazon o'er his towers displayed."

The nearness of kinship implied in the Totem forbade intermarriage; consequently, as husband and wife were of different clans, the Totems were widely dispersed through each Nation. In many of the tribes the Totem, like the chieftainship, descended in the female line, either to a brother born of the same mother, or to a sister's son. The feeling of clanship was as strong among the tribes as it was among the Scotch clans in the time of Rob Roy. If a stranger sought shelter in a village, and found there any one wearing the Totem of his clan, he was sure of safety and assistance.

new treaty was born of greed, and that it held within its folds the germ of a lie."

When the pack-horses were halted upon some uplifted mountain ridge, or upon some rounded upland summit, it was not love for the beauty of this wild, rich nature that looked down upon the fertile glades inclosed within the steep declivities, but the eyes of *Greed*, which cast a covetous glance along the narrow bottom-lands that bordered the winding creeks, and spread into undulating meadows up to the rocky base of the steep and rugged hills. At every such view, Greed dreamed dreams of flocks and herds browsing upon the rich pastures, of waving fields of grain, of wind-blown rows of tasseled corn, of fruitful orchards upon the hillsides, now covered with wooded acres, whose growth outran the centuries that could be counted since the white man's coming.

Upon the borders of Pennsylvania the situation was as threatening as upon the western border of Virginia. The colony of hard-working, hard-fighting, hard-praying, and, as truth is best unveiled, occasionally hard-drinking as well as hard-thinking Scotch-Irish, who began their exodus from Scotland before the fall of the great Montrose and the death of Claverhouse, and who crossed the sea from the North of Ireland to Pennsylvania when the scepter fell from the dead hand of Cromwell, brought into the colony an element altogether different in spirit and action from any then existing there.

The sternest, most set, and determined of all this warlike contingent came over with John Preston, after the siege and loss of Derry made their stay in Ireland impossible.

From the hour of their arrival in the "City of Brotherly Love," detesting the Quakers almost as much as they hated the Church of England or of Rome, they drifted to the west and to the south, to the very outermost boundaries of Pennsylvania and Virginia. Tracing the waters of the Susquehanna and the Potomac to their sources, finding portages across the mountains to the head-waters of the Ohio, they builded their rude wooden citadels upon the extreme verge of the settlements, making for the cautious Dutch emigrants, who followed in their wake, a cordon of defense against the savages upon the border. Clothed with a prickly chain-armor of intolerant beliefs, pestiferous to touch and impossible for defense, believing in the extermination of the Indians in America as they had believed in the extermination of papists at home, and as their New England co-religionists believed in the extermination of witches and Quakers, these fighting sectarists were the advance guard of a fierce, encroaching phalanx, which swept westward, clearing the path of civilization with the besom of extermination.

In their most distorted phase they were monsters of incarnate wrath. In their highest expression of manhood, the world has seen nothing finer, either in character or action. At their worst, cruel and relentless murderers; at their best, they were unselfishly ready to suffer—yes, to welcome death—to save a friend, to establish a principle, to defend a right, or to support and uphold a cause. As if to preserve the contrasting extremes of a race that can best be defined by contrasts, history has sketched the portrait of Simon Girty, and has gilded with martial splendour the story of Stonewall Jackson.

"Penn's policy," as unfolded in his personal dealings with the Indians of Pennsylvania, was eminently just; yet that same "policy," when directed by his successors, covered stupendous frauds in the transfer of Indian lands.

These later purchases were made by the agents through the "Indian Yankees"—the border name for the Iroquois—of the Six Nations, who drove a thrifty trade in lands to which they had not the shadow of ownership. Beginning with the sales of the Delaware lands upon the head-waters of the Susquehanna, the Six Nations continued their fraudulent transactions, until, step by step, the Delawares and the Shawanese were driven back to the Ohio.

The only pretext for this usurpation of authority, was a long-ago conquest of the Delawares (or Tuscaroras) by the then Five Nations, when a final peace was made by the consolidation which introduced the Delawares as an equal power, through their adoption into the Iroquois confederacy, thus changing the number from the "Five" to the "*Six Nations.*"

After their forcible removal from Pennsylvania, the chief settlement of the Delawares was at Logstown, on the right bank of the Ohio, where their king's rule was overshadowed by the arrogant Iroquois sachem Tanacharisen. The Shawanese, originally from South-eastern Georgia and North-western Florida, came north in 1697, and removed from the Susquehanna to the lands upon the north-west tributaries of the Ohio about 1728, when they finally withdrew from the Iroquois confederation. Already allied with the Delawares, both soon formed an alliance with the Miamis.

Immediately after the treaty of Paris, February 10, 1763, the resumption of the interrupted efforts of the original "Ohio Company" to fulfill the conditions of its charter provoked the ill-will and distrust of the Indians upon the Ohio. Organized (in 1748) by the Lees, the Washingtons, and other prominent Virginians, with whom were associated a syndicate of London merchants, its surveys, begun by Christopher Gist, south of the Ohio and east of the Kanawha, had been discontinued during the French and English war; as also had been the surveys of the Loyal Company and the Greenbrier Company. But now there was a general movement westward, and all of these companies were actively pushing their interests, not only upon the head-waters of the Ohio, but their agents in London were asking for further concessions, and for fresh orders of instruction from the Colonial Government at Williamsburg.

All along the frontier the plantations, deserted during the war, were being reoccupied and cultivated. Pioneers were pushing westward to build forts for coming emigrants. Traders were out among the Indian tribes passing from village to village collecting furs and skins.

Into this scene of general activity throughout the Ohio Valley sinister figures were crowding. Grim, sullen warriors gathered around every trading-post, waiting to exchange their peltries for weapons and ammunition. They haughtily turned from "excellent bargains in beads, hand-mirrors, and ornaments," which traders persuasively offered. They would have nothing but "powder and shot," or the gun which was to win for them the trader's goods. The Shawanese and the Delawares were clustering around Fort Pitt. Detached bands of the Miamis were hidden in the wooded dells and sheltered from sight in the forest-shrouded creeks along the banks of the "Beautiful River," watching every canoe and trading-boat that floated upon the "deep, shining water."

The Ottawas, the Ojibways, and the Wyandots had gathered at St. Ignace, ready for the capture of Michilimackinac. Every fort on the lakes and the lake streams was surrounded.

Pontiac, with the bravest bands of the Algonquin Confederacy, was at his village opposite Detroit. The signal of general attack was to be given by Pontiac, and that signal was to be the capture of Detroit. A condensed extract best tells the story of the greatest of the chiefs:

"Among all the wild tribes of the continent personal merit is indispensable to gaining or preserving dignity. Courage, resolution, wisdom, address, and eloquence, are sure passports to distinction. With all these Pontiac was pre-eminently endowed. He possessed commanding energy and force of mind. Capable of acts of lofty magnanimity, he was a thorough savage, with a wider range of intellect than those around him, but sharing all their passions and prejudices. His faults were the faults of his race; and they can not eclipse his noble qualities, the great powers and heroic virtues of his mind. His memory is still cherished among the remnants of many Algonquin tribes, and the celebrated Tecumseh adopted him for his model, proving himself no unworthy imitator.

"During the war he had fought on the side of France. It is said that he commanded the Ottawas at the memorable defeat of Braddock.

"When the tide of affairs changed the subtle and ambitious chief trimmed his bark to the current, and gave the hand of friendship to the English. That he was disappointed in their treatment of him, and in all the hopes that he had formed from their alliance, is sufficiently evident from one of his speeches.

"It was a momentous and gloomy crisis for the Indian race, for never before had they been exposed to such pressing and imminent danger.

"The English had gained an undisputed ascendency, and the Indians, no longer important as allies, were treated as mere barbarians, who might be trampled upon with impunity.

"Already their best hunting-grounds were invaded, and from the eastern ridges of the Alleghanies they might see, from far and near, the smoke of the settler's clearings.

"Goaded by wrongs and indignities, they struck for revenge and relief from the evil of the moment. But the mind of Pontiac could embrace a wider and deeper view. The peril of the times was unfolded in its full extent before him, and he resolved to unite the tribes in one grand effort to avert it. He adopted the only plan that was consistent with reason, that of restoring the French ascendency in the West, and once more opposing a check to British encroachment.

"Revenge, ambition, and patriotism wrought upon him alike, and he resolved on war. At the close of the year 1762 he sent out ambassadors to the different nations. They visited the country of the Ohio and its tributaries, passed northward to the region of the upper lakes and the wild borders of the River Ottawa, and far southward towards the mouth of the Mississippi. Bearing with them the war-belt of wampum, broad and long, as the importance of the message demanded, and the tomahawk stained red, in token of war, they went from camp to camp, and village to village. Wherever they appeared the sachems and old men assembled, to hear the words of the great Pontiac. Then the head chief of the embassy flung down the tomahawk on the ground before them, and, holding the war-belt in his hand, delivered, with vehement gesture, word for word, the speech with which he was charged. It was heard everywhere with approbation, the belt was accepted, the hatchet snatched up, and the assembled chiefs stood pledged to take part in the war. The blow was to be struck at a certain time in the month of May following, to be indicated by the changes of the moon. The tribes were to rise together, each destroying the English garrison in its neighborhood, and then, with a general rush, the whole were to turn against the settlements of the frontier.

"While thus on the very eve of an outbreak, the Indians concealed their design with the deep dissimulation of their race. Now and then some slight intimation of danger would startle the garrisons from their security. On one occasion the plot was nearly discovered. Early in March, 1763, Ensign Holmes, commanding at Fort Miami, was told by a friendly Indian that the warriors in the neighboring village had lately received a war-belt, with a message urging them to destroy him and his garrison, and that this they were preparing to do. Holmes writes to report his discovery to Major Gladwyn, who, in his turn, sends the information to Sir Jeffrey Amherst, expressing his opinion that there has been a general irritation among the Indians, but that the affair will soon blow over, and that, in the neighborhood of his own post, the savages were perfectly tranquil. Within cannon-shot of the deluded officer's palisades was the village of Pontiac himself.

"While the war was on the eve of breaking out, an event occurred which had afterwards an important effect upon its progress, the signing of the treaty of peace at Paris, on the 10th of February, 1763. By this treaty

France resigned her claims to the territories east of the Mississippi, and that great river now became the western boundary of the British colonial possessions. England left the valley of the Ohio and the adjacent regions as an Indian domain, and, by the proclamation of the 7th of October following, the intrusion of settlers upon these lands was strictly prohibited. But the remedy came too late. While the sovereigns of France, England, and Spain were signing the treaty at Paris, countless Indian warriors in the American forests were singing the war-song and whetting their scalping-knives.

"The council took place on the 27th of April. On that morning several old men, the heralds of the camp, passed to and fro among the lodges, calling the warriors, in a loud voice, to attend the meeting.

"All were soon seated in a wide circle upon the grass, row within row, a grave and silent assembly. Pipes, with ornamented stems, were lighted, and passed from hand to hand.

"Then Pontiac rose, and walked forward into the midst of the council, plumed and painted in the full panoply of war. Looking round upon his wild auditors, he began to speak, with fierce gesture, and loud, impassioned voice; and at every pause, deep guttural ejaculations of assent and approval responded to his words. He inveighed against the arrogance, rapacity, and injustice of the English, and contrasted them with the French, whom they had driven from the soil. He represented the danger that would arise from the supremacy of the English. Then holding out a broad belt of wampum, he told the council that he had received it from their great father, the king of France, in token that he had heard the voice of his red children; that his sleep was at an end; and that his great war-canoes would soon sail up the St. Lawrence, to win back Canada, and wreak vengeance on his enemies. The Indians and their French brethren should fight once more, side by side, as they had always fought; they should strike the English as they had struck them many moons ago, when their great army marched down the Monongahela, and they had shot them from their ambush, like a flock of pigeons in the woods.

"Having roused in his warlike listeners their native thirst for blood and vengeance, he next addressed himself to their superstition.

"Pontiac told them, in conclusion, that on the 2d of May he would gain admittance, with a party of his warriors, on pretense of dancing the Calumet dance before the garrison; that they would take note of the strength of the fortification; and, this information gained, he would summon another council to determine the mode of attack.

"On the 1st of May Pontiac came to the gate with forty men of the Ottawa tribe, and asked permission to enter and dance the Calumet dance before the officers of the garrison. After some hesitation he was admitted, and proceeding to the corner of the street where stood the house of the commandant, Major Gladwyn, he and thirty of his warriors began their dance, each recounting his own valiant exploits, and boasting himself the bravest of mankind. The officers and men gathered around them; while, in the meantime, the remaining ten of the Ottawas strolled about the fort, observing every thing it contained. When the dance was over, they all quietly withdrew, not a suspicion of their sinister design having arisen in the minds of the English.

"After a few days had elapsed, Pontiac's messengers again passed among the Indian cabins, calling the principal chiefs to another council in the Pottawattamie village. He once more addressed the chiefs, inciting them to hostility against the English, and concluded by the proposal of his plan for destroying Detroit.

"On the afternoon of the 5th of May, a Canadian woman, the wife of Lieutenant Aubin, one of the principal settlers, crossed over from the western side, and visited the Ottawa village, to obtain from the Indians a supply of maple-sugar and venison. She was surprised at finding several of the warriors engaged in filing off the muzzles of their guns, so as to reduce them, stock and all, to the length of about a yard.

"Returning home in the evening, she mentioned what she had seen to several of her neighbors. Upon this, one of them, the blacksmith of the village, remarked that many of the Indians had lately visited his shop, and attempted to borrow files and saws for a purpose which they would not explain. These circumstances excited the suspicion of the experienced Canadians. M. Gouin, an old and wealthy settler, went to the commandant and conjured him to stand upon his guard; but Gladwyn, a man of fearless temper, gave no heed to the friendly advice.

"In the Pottawattamie village lived an Ojibway girl, who, if there be truth in tradition, could boast a larger share of beauty than is common in the wigwam. She had attracted the eye of Gladwyn, and she had become much attached to him. On the afternoon of the 6th, Catharine—for so the officers called her—came to the fort, and repaired to Gladwyn's quarters, bringing with her a pair of elk-skin moccasins, ornamented with porcupine work, which he had requested her to make. There was something unusual in her look and manner. Her face was sad and downcast. She said little, and soon left the room; but the sentinel at the door saw her still lingering at the street corner, though the hour for closing the gates was nearly come. At length she attracted the notice of Gladwyn himself; and calling to her, he pressed her to declare what was weighing upon her mind. Still she remained for a long time silent, and it was only after much urgency and many promises not to betray her, that she revealed her momentous secret.

"'To-morrow,' she said, 'Pontiac will come to the fort with sixty of his chiefs, each will be armed with a gun, cut short, and hidden under his blanket. Pontiac will demand to hold a council; and after he has delivered his speech, he will offer a peace-belt of wampum, holding it in a reversed position. This will be the signal of attack. The chiefs will spring up and fire upon the officers, and the Indians in the street will fall upon the garrison. Every Englishman will be killed, but not the scalp of a single Frenchman will be touched.'

"Gladwyn was an officer of signal courage and address. Calling his subordinates together, he imparted what he had heard. Every preparation was made to meet the sudden emergency. Half the garrison were ordered under arms, and all the officers prepared to spend the night upon the ramparts. 'It rained all day,' writes the chronicler, ' but cleared up towards evening, and there was a very fair sunset.'

"From sunset till dawn an anxious watch was kept from the slender palisades of Detroit. The soldiers were still ignorant of the danger, and the sentinels did not know why their numbers were doubled, or why, with such unwonted vigilance, their officers visited their posts. Again and again Gladwyn mounted his wooden ramparts and looked forth into the gloom. There seemed nothing but repose and peace in the soft, moist air; but at intervals, as the night wind swept across the bastion it bore sounds of fearful portent to the ear, the sullen booming of the Indian drum and the wild chorus of quavering yells, as the warriors, around their distant camp-fires, danced the war-dance in preparation for the morrow's work.

"The sun rose upon fresh fields and newly budding woods, and scarcely had the morning mists dissolved, when the garrison could see a fleet of birch canoes crossing the river from the eastern shore, within range of cannon-shot above the fort. Only two or three warriors appeared in each, but all moved slowly, and seemed deeply laden. In truth, they were full of savages lying flat on their faces, that their number might not excite the suspicion of the English.

"At an early hour the open common behind the fort was thronged with squaws, children, and warriors, some naked, and others fantastically arrayed in their barbarous finery. All seemed restless and uneasy, moving hither and thither, in apparent preparation for a general game of ball. Then, with an air of assumed indifference, they would move towards the gate. They were all admitted, for Gladwyn who, in this instance, at least, showed some knowledge of Indian character, chose to convince his crafty foe that, though their plot was detected, their hostility was despised.

"At ten o'clock the great war chief, with his treacherous followers, reached the fort, and the gateway was thronged with their savage faces. All were wrapped to the throat in colored blankets. Some were crested with hawk, eagle, or raven plumes; others had shaved their heads, leaving only the fluttering scalp-lock on the crown. For the most part they were tall, strong men, and all had a gait and bearing of peculiar stateliness.

"As Pontiac entered it is said that he started, and that a deep ejaculation half escaped from his broad chest. On either hand, within the gateway, stood ranks of soldiers and hedges of glittering steel. The swarthy, half-wild *engagés* of the fur-traders, armed to the teeth, stood in groups at the street corner, and the measured tap of a drum fell ominously on the ear. Pontiac strode forward into the narrow street, and his chiefs filed after him in silence. Their rigid muscles betrayed no sign of emotion; yet, looking closely, one might have seen their small eyes glance from side to side with restless scrutiny.

"Traversing the entire width of the little town, they reached the door of the council-house, a large building standing near the margin of the river. Entering, they saw Gladwyn with several of his officers seated in readiness to receive them, and the observant chiefs did not fail to remark that every Englishman wore a sword at his side and a pair of pistols in his belt. The conspirators eyed each other with uneasy glances. 'Why,' demanded Pontiac, ' do I see so many of my father's young men standing in the street with their guns?' Gladwyn replied through his interpreter, La Butte, that he had ordered the soldiers under arms for the sake of exercise and discipline. With much delay and many signs of disgust the chiefs at length sat down on the mats prepared for them, and after the customary pause, Pontiac rose to speak. Holding in his hand the wampum-belt, which was to have given the fatal signal, he addressed the commandant, professing strong attachment to the English, and declaring, in Indian phrase, that he had come to smoke the pipe of peace and brighten the chain of friendship. The officers watched him keenly as he uttered these hollow words, and once, it is said, he raised the wampum-belt as if about to give the signal of attack. But, at that instant, Gladwyn signed slightly with his hand. The sudden clash of arms sounded from the passage without, and a drum rolling the charge filled the council-room with its stunning din. At this Pontiac stood like one confounded, and soon sat down in amazement and perplexity.

"Another pause ensued, and Gladwyn commenced a brief reply. He assured the chiefs that friendship and protection should be extended towards them as long as they continued to deserve it, but threatened ample vengeance for the first act of aggression. The council then broke up; but before leaving the room Pontiac told the officers that he would return in a few days, with his squaws and children, for he wished that they should all shake hands with their fathers, the English. To this new piece of treachery Gladwyn deigned no reply. The gates of the fort, which had been closed during the conference, were again flung open, and the baffled savages were suffered to depart.

"Balked in his treachery, the great chief withdrew to his village, enraged and mortified, yet still resolved to persevere. That Gladwyn had suffered him to escape, was to his mind an ample proof either of cowardice or ignorance. The latter supposition seemed the more probable, and he resolved to visit the English once more, and convince them, if possible, that their suspicions were unfounded. Early on the following morning he repaired to the fort with three of his chiefs, bearing in his hand the sacred calumet, or pipe of peace, the bowl carved in stone and the stem adorned with feathers. Offering it to the commandant, he addressed him and his officers: 'My fathers, evil birds have sung lies in your ear. We that stand before you are friends of the English. We love them as our brothers, and, to prove our love, we have come this day to smoke the pipe of peace.'

"At his departure he gave the pipe to Major Campbell, second in command, as a farther pledge of his sincerity.

"Early on the following morning, Monday, the 9th of May, before eleven o'clock, the common behind the fort was once more thronged with Indians of all the four tribes; and Pontiac, advancing from among the multitude, approached the gate. It was closed and barred against him. Pontiac shouted to the sentinels, and demanded why he was refused admittance. Gladwyn himself replied that the great chief might enter, if he chose, but that the crowd he had brought with him must remain outside. Pontiac rejoined that he wished all his warriors to enjoy the fragrance of the friendly calumet. Gladwyn's answer was more concise than courteous, and imported that he would have none of his rabble in the fort. Thus repulsed, Pontiac threw off the mask which he had worn so long; he turned abruptly from the gate and strode towards his followers, who in great multitudes lay flat upon the ground, just beyond reach of gunshot. At his approach they all leaped up and ran off, yelping, in the words of an eye-witness, like so many devils.

"Looking out from the loop-holes, the garrison could see them running in a body towards the house of an old English woman, who lived, with her family, on a distant part of the common. They beat down the doors and rushed tumultuously in. A moment more and the mournful scalp-yell told the fate of the wretched inmates.

"During the evening fresh tidings of disaster reached the fort. A Canadian, named Desnoyers, came down the river in a birch canoe, and, landing at the water-gate, brought news that two English officers, Sir Robert Davies and Captain Robertson, had been waylaid and murdered by the Indians, above Lake St. Clair. The Canadians declared, moreover, that Pontiac had just been joined by a formidable band of Ojibways, from the Bay of Saginaw.

"Every Englishman in the fort, whether trader or soldier, was now ordered under arms. No man lay down to sleep, and Gladwyn himself walked the ramparts throughout the night.

"All was quiet till the approach of dawn. But as the first dim redness tinged the east, and fields and woods grew visible in the morning twilight, suddenly the war-whoop rose on every side at once. Indians, pealing their terrific yells, came bounding naked to the assault. The soldiers looked from the loop-holes, thinking to see their assailants gathering for a rush against the feeble barrier. But, though their clamors filled the air, and their guns blazed thick and hot, yet very few were visible.

"There was one low hill, at no great distance from the fort, behind which countless black heads of Indians alternately appeared and vanished, while all along the ridge their guns emitted incessant white puffs of smoke. Every loop-hole was a target for their bullets; but the fire was returned with steadiness, and not without effect. The Canadian *engagés* of the fur-traders retorted the Indian war-whoops with outcries not less discordant, while the British and provincials paid back the clamor of the enemy with musket and rifle balls. Within half gunshot of the palisade was a cluster of out-buildings, behind which a host of Indians found shelter. A cannon was brought to bear upon them, loaded with red-hot spikes. They were soon wrapped in flames, upon which the disconcerted savages broke away in a body, and ran off yelping, followed by a shout of laughter from the soldiers.

"For six hours the attack was unabated; but as the day advanced the assailants grew weary of their futile efforts. Their fire slackened, their clamors died away, and the garrison was left once more in peace, though from time to time a solitary shot, or lonely whoop, still showed the presence of some lingering savage, loath to be balked of his revenge. Among the garrison only five men had been wounded, while the cautious enemy had suffered but trifling loss.

"Gladwyn was still convinced that the whole affair was but a sudden ebullition, which would soon subside; and being, moreover, in great want of provision, he resolved to open negotiations with the Indians. The interpreter, La Butte, was dispatched to the camp of Pontiac, to demand the reasons of his conduct, and declare that the commandant was ready to redress any real grievance of which he might complain. Two old Canadians, of Detroit, Chapeton and Godefroy, earnest to forward the negotiations, offered to accompany him.

"Reaching the Indian camp, the three ambassadors were received by Pontiac with great apparent kindness. La Butte delivered his message, and the two Canadians labored to dissuade the chief, for his own good and for theirs, from pursuing his hostile purposes. Pontiac stood listening, armed with the true impenetrability of an Indian. Yet with all this seeming acquiescence, the heart of the savage was unmoved as a rock. The Canadians were completely deceived.

"At La Butte's appearance all the chiefs withdrew to consult among themselves. They returned after a short debate, and Pontiac declared that, out of their earnest desire for firm and lasting peace, they wished to hold council with their English fathers themselves. With this view, they were expressly desirous that Major Campbell, second in command, should visit their camp. This veteran officer, from his just, upright, and manly character, had gained the confidence of the Indians. To the Canadians the proposal seemed a natural one, and, returning to the fort, they laid it before the commandent. Gladwyn suspected treachery, but Major Campbell urgently asked permission to comply with the request of Pontiac. He felt, he said, no fear of the Indians, with whom he had always maintained the most friendly terms. Gladwyn, with some hesitation, acceded, and Campbell left the fort, accompanied by a junior officer, Lieutenant McDougal, and attended by La Butte and several other Canadians.

"In the meantime Mr. Gouin, anxious to learn what was passing, had entered the Indian camp, and, moving from lodge to lodge, soon saw and heard enough to convince him that the two British officers were advancing into the lion's jaws. He hastened to dispatch two messengers to warn them of the peril. The party had scarcely left the gate, when they were met by these men, breathless with running; but the warning came too late. Once embarked on the embassy, the officers would not be diverted from it; and passing up the river road, they approached the little wooden bridge that led over Parent's Creek. Crossing this bridge, and ascending a rising ground beyond, they saw before them the wide-spread camp of the Ottawas. A dark multitude gathered along its outskirts, and no sooner did they recognize the red uniform of the officers, than they all raised at once a horrible outcry of whoops and howlings. Indeed, they seemed disposed to give the ambassadors the reception usually accorded to captives taken in war; for the women seized sticks, stones, and clubs, and ran towards Campbell and his companions, as if to make them pass the cruel ordeal of running the gauntlet. Pontiac came forward, and his voice allayed the tumult. He shook the officers by the hand, and turning, led the way through the camp. He paused before the entrance of a large lodge, and, entering, pointed to several mats placed on the ground at the side opposite the opening. Here, obedient to his signal, the two officers sat down. Instantly the lodge was thronged with savages. At their entrance, Pontiac had spoken a few words. A pause then ensued, broken at length by Campbell, who from his seat addressed the Indians in a short speech. It was heard in perfect silence, and no reply was made. At length Major Campbell, conscious, no doubt, of the danger in which he was placed, resolved fully to ascertain his true position, and rising to his feet, declared his intention of returning to the fort. Pontiac made a sign that he should resume his seat. 'My father,' he said, 'will sleep to-night in the lodges of his red children.' The gray-haired soldier and his companion were betrayed into the hands of their enemies.

"Many of the Indians were eager to kill the captives on the spot, but Pontiac would not carry his treachery so far.

"On the morning after the detention of the officers, Pontiac crossed over, with several of his chiefs, to the Wyandot village. A part of this tribe, influenced by Father Pothier, their Jesuit priest, had refused to take up arms against the English; but being now threatened with destruction if they should longer remain neutral, they were forced to join the rest. Having secured these new allies, Pontiac prepared to resume his operations with fresh vigor. On the 12th of May, when these arrangements were complete, the Indians once more surrounded the fort, firing upon it from morning till night.

"On the evening of that day, the officers met to consider what course of conduct the emergency required; and, as one of them writes, the commandant was almost alone in his opinion that they ought still to defend the place.

"Day after day the Indians continued their attacks, until their war-cries and the rattle of their guns became familiar sounds.

"For many weeks no man lay down to sleep except in his clothes, and with his weapons by his side. Parties of volunteers sallied, from time to time, to burn the out-buildings, which gave shelter to the enemy. They cut down orchard trees, and leveled fences, until the ground about the fort was clear and open, and the enemy had no cover left from whence to fire. The two vessels in the river, sweeping the northern and southern curtains of the works with their fire, deterred the Indians from approaching those points, and gave material aid to the garrison. Soon after the first attack, the Ottawa chief had sent in to Gladwyn a summons to surrender, assuring him that if the place were at once given up, he might embark on board the vessels, with all his men; but that, if he persisted in his defense, he would treat him as Indians treat each other; that is, he would burn him alive. To this Gladwyn made answer that he cared nothing for his threats. The attacks were now renewed with increased activity, and the assailants were soon after inspired with fresh ardor by the arrival of a hundred and twenty Ojibway warriors from Grand River.

"Detroit must have been abandoned or destroyed, but for the assistance of a few friendly Canadians, and especially of M. Baby, a prominent *habitant*, who lived on the opposite side of the river, and provided the garrison with cattle, hogs, and other supplies.

"Major Rogers, a man familiar with the Indians, and an acute judge of mankind, speaks in the highest terms of Pontiac's character and talents. 'He puts on,' he says, 'an air of majesty and princely grandeur, and is greatly honored and revered by his subjects.'

"Pontiac had sent messengers to M. Neyon, commandant at the Illinois, earnestly requesting that a force of regular troops might be sent to his assistance; and Gladwyn, on his side, had ordered one of the vessels to Niagara, to hasten forward the expected convoy. The schooner set sail, but on the next day, as she lay becalmed at the entrance of Lake Erie, a multitude of canoes suddenly darted out upon her from the neighboring shores. In the prow of the foremost the Indians had placed their prisoner, Major Campbell, with the dastardly purpose of interposing him as a screen between themselves and the fire of the English. But the brave old man called out to the crew to do their duty, without regard to him. Happily, at that moment a fresh breeze sprang up; the flapping sails stretched to the wind, and the schooner bore prosperously on her course toward Niagara, leaving the savage flotilla far behind.

"On the 30th of May, at about nine o'clock, the voice of the sentinel sounded from the south-east bastion, and loud exclamations, in the direction of the river, roused Detroit from its lethargy. Instantly the place was astir. The long-expected convoy was full in sight. On the further side of the river, at some distance below the fort, a line of boats was rounding the woody projection, then called Montreal Point, their oars flashing in the sun, and the red flag of England flying from the stern of the foremost. The toils and dangers of the garrison were drawing to an end. With one accord they broke into three hearty cheers, again and again repeated, while a cannon, glancing from the bastion, sent its loud voice of defiance to the enemy, and welcome to approaching friends. But suddenly every cheek grew pale with horror. Dark, naked figures were seen rising, with wild gesture, in the boats, while, in the place of the answering salute, the distant yell of the war-whoop fell faintly on their ears. The convoy was in the hands of the enemy. The boats had all been taken, and the troops of the detachment slain or made captive. Officers and men stood gazing in a mournful silence, when an incident occurred which caused them to forget the general calamity in the absorbing interest of the moment.

"In each of the boats, of which there were eighteen, two or more of the captured soldiers, deprived of their weapons, were compelled to act as rowers, guarded by several armed savages, while many other Indians, for the sake of farther security, followed the boats along the shore. In the foremost, as it happened, there were four soldiers and only three Indians. The larger of the two vessels still lay anchored in the stream, about a bow-shot from the fort, while her companion, as we have seen, had gone down to Niagara to hasten up this very re-enforcement. As the boat came opposite this vessel the soldier who acted as steersman conceived a daring plan of escape. The principal Indian sat immediately in front of another of the soldiers. The steersman called, in English, to his comrade to seize the savage and throw him overboard. The man answered that he was not strong enough, on which the steersman directed him to change places with him, as if fatigued with rowing, a movement which would excite no suspicion on the part of the guard. As the bold soldier stepped forward, as if to take his companion's oar, he suddenly seized the Indian by the hair, and gripping with the other hand the girdle at his waist, lifted him by main force, and flung him into the river. The boat rocked till the water surged over her gunwale. The Indian held fast to his enemy's clothes, and drawing himself upwards as he trailed alongside, stabbed him again and again with his knife, and then dragged him overboard. Both went down the swift current, rising and sinking, and, as some relate, perished, grappled in each other's arms. The two remaining Indians leaped out of the boat. The prisoners turned and pulled for the distant vessel, shouting aloud for aid. The Indians on shore opened a heavy fire upon them, and many canoes paddled swiftly in pursuit. The men strained with desperate strength. A fate inexpressibly horrible was the alternative. The bullets hissed thickly around their heads; one of them was soon wounded, and the light birch canoes gained on them with fearful rapidity. Escape seemed hopeless, when the report of a cannon burst from the side of the vessel. The ball flew close past the boat, beating the water in a line of foam, and narrowly missing the foremost canoe. At this the pursuers drew back in dismay; and the Indians on shore, being farther saluted by a second shot, ceased firing, and scattered among the bushes. The prisoners soon reached the vessel, when they were greeted as men snatched from the jaws of fate. 'A living monument,' writes an officer of the garrison, 'that fortune favors the brave.'

"After night had set in several Canadians came to the fort bringing vague and awful reports of the scenes that had been enacted at the Indian camp. The soldiers gathered round them, and, frozen with horror, listened to the appalling narrative. On the following day, and for several succeeding days, they beheld frightful confirmation of the rumors they had heard. Naked corpses, gashed with knives and scorched with fire, floated down on the pure waters of the Detroit, whose fish came up to nibble at the clotted blood that clung to their ghastly faces.

"Late one afternoon, at about this period of the siege, the garrison were again greeted with the dismal cry of death, and a line of naked warriors were seen issuing from the woods, which, like a wall of foliage, rose beyond the pastures in rear of the fort. Each savage was painted black, and each bore a scalp fluttering from the end of a pole. It was but too clear that some new disaster had befallen; and in truth, before nightfall, one La Brosse, a Canadian, came to the gate with the tidings that Fort Sandusky had been taken, and all its garrison slain or made captive. Among the few survivors of the slaughter was the commanding officer, Ensign Paully, who had been brought prisoner to Detroit, bound hand and foot, and solaced on the passage with the expectation of being burnt alive; but an old woman, whose husband had lately died, chose to adopt him in place of the deceased warrior. Seeing no alternative but the stake, Paully accepted the proposal; and having been first plunged in the river, that the white blood might be washed from his veins, he was conducted to the lodge of the widow, and treated thenceforth with all the consideration due to an Ottawa warrior.

"Gladwyn soon received a letter from him, through one of the Canadian inhabitants, giving a full account of Fort Sandusky. On the 16th of May—such was the substance of the communication—Paully was informed that seven Indians were waiting at the gate to speak with him. As several of the number were well known to him, he ordered them, without hesitation, to be admitted. Arrived at his quarters, two of the treacherous visitors seated themselves on each side of the commandant, while the rest were dispersed in various parts of the room. The pipes were lighted, and the conversation began, when an Indian, who stood in the doorway, suddenly made a signal by raising his head. Upon this, the astonished officer was instantly pounced upon and disarmed; while, at the same moment, a confused noise of shrieks and yells, the firing of guns, and the hurried tramp of feet, sounded from the area of the fort without. It soon ceased, however, and Paully, led by his captors from the room, saw the parade-ground strewn with the corpses of his murdered garrison. At night-fall, he was conducted to the margin of the lake, where several birch canoes lay in readiness, and as, amid thick darkness, the party pushed out from shore, the captive saw the fort, lately under his command, bursting on all sides into sheets of flame.

"The sleepless garrison, worn by fatigue and ill-fare, and harassed by constant petty attacks, were yet further saddened by the news of disaster which thickened from every quarter. Of all the small posts, scattered at wide intervals through the vast wilderness to the westward of Niagara and Fort Pitt, it soon appeared that Detroit alone had been able to sustain itself. For the rest, there was but one unvaried tale of calamity and ruin. On the 15th of June, a number of Pottawattamies were seen approaching the gate of the fort, bringing with them four English prisoners, who proved to be Ensign Schlosser, lately commanding at St. Joseph's, together with three private soldiers. The Indians wished to exchange them for several of their own tribe, who had been for nearly two months prisoners in the fort. After some delay this was effected, and the garrison then learned the unhappy fate of their comrades at St. Joseph's.

"The next news which came in was that of the loss of Ouatanon, a fort situated upon the Wabash, a little below the site of the present town of Lafayette. Gladwyn received a letter from its commanding officer, Lieutenant Jenkins, informing him that, on the 1st of June, he and several of his men had been made prisoners by stratagem, on which the rest of the garrison had surrendered. The Indians, however, apologized for their conduct, declaring that they acted contrary to their own inclinations, and that the surrounding tribes had compelled them to take up the hatchet.

"Close upon these tidings came the news that Fort Miami was taken. This post, standing on the River Maumee, was commanded by Ensign Holmes.

"The loss of Presque Isle will close this black catalogue of calamity. Rumors of it first reached Detroit on the 20th of June, and two days later the garrison heard those dismal cries, announcing scalps and prisoners, which, of late, had grown mournfully familiar to their ears. Indians were

INDIAN CONFLICTS.

seen passing in numbers along the opposite bank of the river, leading several English prisoners, who proved to be Ensign Christie, the commanding officer at Presque Isle, with those of his soldiers who survived. There had been hot fighting before Presque Isle was taken.

"At early dawn on the 15th of June the garrison of Presque Isle were first aware of the enemy's presence; and when the sun rose they saw themselves surrounded by two hundred Indians, chiefly from the neighborhood of Detroit. At the first alarm they abandoned the main body of the fort, and betook themselves to the block-house as a citadel. The Indians crowding together in great numbers, under cover of the rising ground, kept up a rattling fire, and not only sent their bullets into every loop-hole and crevice, but shot fire-arrows upon the roof, and threw balls of burning pitch against the walls. Again and again the building took fire, and again and again the flames were extinguished. From earliest daybreak the little garrison had fought and toiled without a moment's rest. Nor did the darkness bring relief, for guns flashed all night long from the Indian intrenchments. Morning brought fresh dangers. The men were now, to use the words of their officer, 'exhausted to the greatest extremity;' yet they kept up their forlorn and desperate defense, toiling and fighting without pause within the wooden walls of their dark prison, where the close and heated atmosphere was clogged with the smoke of gunpowder. The fire on both sides continued through the day, and did not cease till midnight, at which hour a voice was heard to call out in French, from the enemy's intrenchments, warning the garrison that further resistance would be useless, since preparations were made for setting the block-house on fire. Christie demanded if there were any among them who spoke English; upon which a man in the Indian dress came out from behind the breastwork. He said that if they yielded their lives should be spared, but if they fought longer they must all be burnt alive. Christie, resolving to hold out as long as a shadow of hope remained, told them to wait till morning for his answer. When morning came Christie sent out two soldiers, as if to treat with the enemy, but, in reality, to learn the truth of what they had said respecting their preparations to burn the block-house. On reaching the breastwork the soldiers made a signal, by which their officer saw that his worst fears were well founded, and Christie, going out, yielded up the little fortress which he had defended with such indomitable courage, having first stipulated that the lives of all the garrison should be spared, and that they might retire unmolested to the nearest post. The soldiers, pale, wild, and haggard, like men who had passed through a fiery ordeal, now issued from the block-house, whose sides were pierced with bullets and scorched with fire. In spite of the capitulation, they were surrounded and seized, and having been detained for some time in the neighborhood, were sent as prisoners to Detroit, where Ensign Christie soon after made his escape, and gained the fort in safety.

"After Presque Isle was taken, the neighboring little posts of Le Bœuf and Venango shared its fate, while farther southward, at the forks of the Ohio, a host of Delaware and Shawanese warriors were gathering around Fort Pitt, and blood and havoc reigned along the whole frontier.

"On the 19th of June a rumor reached them, at Detroit, that one of the vessels had been seen near Turkey Island, some miles below the fort, but that, the wind failing her, she had dropped down with the current, to wait a more favorable opportunity.

"For several days the officers at Detroit heard nothing further of the vessel, when, on the 23d, a great commotion was visible among the Indians. The cause of these movements was unknown till evening, when M. Baby came in with intelligence that the vessel was again attempting to ascend the river, and that all the Indians had gone to attack her. Upon this two cannon were fired, that those on board might know that the fort still held out.

"The schooner brought to the garrison a much needed supply of men, ammunition, and provision. She brought, also, the interesting and important tidings that peace was at length concluded between France and England. By this treaty the Canadians of Detroit were placed in a new position; their allegiance was transferred from the crown of France to that of Britain, and they were subjects of the English king. To many of them the change was extremely odious, for they cordially hated the British. They went about among the settlers and the Indians, declaring that the pretended news of peace was only an invention of Major Gladwyn; that the king of France would never abandon his children. This oft-repeated falsehood was implicitly believed by the Indians.

"Pontiac himself clung fast to this delusive hope. He exerted himself with fresh zeal to gain possession of the place, and attempted to terrify Gladwyn into submission. He sent a message, in which he strongly urged him to surrender, adding, by way of stimulus, that eight hundred more

Ojibways were every day expected, and that, on their arrival, all his influence could not prevent them from taking the scalp of every Englishman in the fort. To this friendly advice Gladwyn returned a very brief and contemptuous answer.

"Pontiac, having long been anxious to gain the Canadians as auxiliaries in the war, now determined on a final effort to effect his object. For this purpose he sent messages to the principal inhabitants, inviting them to meet him in council. In the Ottawa camp there was a vacant spot, quite level, and encircled by the huts of the Indians. Here mats were spread for the reception of the deputies, who soon convened, and took their seats in a wide ring. One part was occupied by the Canadians, among whom were several whose withered, leathery features proclaimed them the patriarchs of the secluded little settlement. Opposite these sat the stern-visaged Pontiac, with his chiefs on either hand, while the intervening portions of the circle were filled by Canadians and Indians promiscuously mingled. Standing on the outside, and looking over the heads of this more dignified assemblage, was a motley throng of Indians and Canadians, half-breeds, trappers, and voyageurs, in wild and picturesque, though very dirty, attire. Conspicuous among them were numerous Indian dandies, a large class in every aboriginal community.

"All was silent, and several pipes were passing round from hand to hand, when Pontiac rose and threw down a war-belt at the feet of the Canadians.

"'My brothers,' he said 'how long will you suffer this bad flesh to remain upon your lands? I have told you before, and I now tell you again, that when I took up the hatchet, it was for your good. This year the English must all perish throughout Canada. Until now I have said nothing on this matter. I have not urged you to take part with us in the war. It would have been enough had you been content to sit quiet on your mats, looking on, while we were fighting for you; but you have have not done so. You call yourself our friends, and yet you assist the English with provision, and go about as spies among our villages. This must not continue. You must be either wholly French or wholly English. If you are French, take up that war-belt and lift the hatchet with us; but if you are English, then we declare war upon you. Look upon the belt, and let us hear your answer.'

"One of the Canadians, having suspected the purpose of Pontiac, had brought with him, not the treaty of peace, but a copy of the capitulation of

Montreal, with its dependencies, including Detroit. Pride, or some other motive, restrained him from confessing that the Canadians were no longer children of the king of France, and he determined to keep up the old delusion that a French army was on its way to win back Canada, and chastise the English invaders. He began his speech in reply to Pontiac by professing great love for the Indians, and a strong desire to aid them in the war. 'But, my brothers,' he added, holding out the articles of capitulation, 'you must first untie the knot with which our great father, the king, has bound us. In this paper he tells all his Canadian children to sit quiet and obey the English until he comes. We dare not disobey him. Do you think you could escape his wrath if you should raise the hatchet against his French children? Tell us, my brothers, what can you reply to this?'

"Pontiac for a moment sat silent, mortified, and perplexed; but his purpose was not destined to be wholly defeated. 'Among the French,' says the writer of the diary, 'were many infamous characters, who, having no property, cared nothing what became of them.' They were, for the most part, a light and frivolous crew, little to be relied on for energy or stability; though among them were men of hard and ruffian features, the ringleaders and bullies of the *voyageurs*, and even a terror to the bourgeois himself. It was one of these who now took up the war-belt, and declared that he and his comrades were ready to raise the hatchet for Pontiac. The council had been protracted to a late hour. It was dark before the assembly dissolved; 'so that,' as the chronicler observes, 'these new Indians had no opportunity of displaying their exploits that day.'

"Pontiac derived little advantage from his Canadian allies. On the night succeeding the feast a party of the renegades, joined by about an equal number of Indians, approached the fort. They were observed, the gate was thrown open, and a file of men, headed by Lieutenant Hay, sallied out to dislodge them. This was effected without much difficulty.

"Until the end of July, little worthy of notice took place at Detroit. In the meantime, unknown to the garrison, a strong re-enforcement was coming to their aid. Captain Dalzell had left Niagara with twenty-two barges, bearing two hundred and eighty men, with several small cannon, and a fresh supply of provision and ammunition.

"On the day of his arrival he had a conference with Gladwyn at the quarters of the latter, and strongly insisted that the time was come when an irrecoverable blow might be struck at Pontiac. He requested permission to march out on the following night and attack the Indian camp. Gladwyn, better acquainted with the position of affairs, and, perhaps, more cautious by nature, was averse to the attempt; but Dalzell urged his request so strenuously that the commandant yielded to his representation, and gave a tardy consent. On the afternoon of the 30th orders were issued and preparations made for the meditated attack.

"About two o'clock, on the morning of the 31st of July, the gates were thrown open in silence, and the detachment, two hundred and fifty in number, passed noiselessly out.

"A mile and a half from the fort, Parent's Creek, ever since that night called 'Bloody Run,' descended through a wild and rough hollow, and entered the Detroit amid a growth of rank grass and sedge. Only a few rods from its mouth the road crossed it by a narrow wooden bridge, not existing at the present day. The advanced guard were half-way over the bridge, and the main body just entering upon it, when a horrible burst of yells rose in their front, and the Indian guns blazed forth a general discharge. Half the advanced party were shot down; but Dalzell shouted from the van, and, in madness of mingled rage and fear, they charged at a run across the bridge and up the heights beyond. Not an Indian was there to oppose them. In vain the furious soldiers sought their enemy behind fences and intrenchments. The active savages had fled; yet still their guns flashed thick through the gloom, and their war-cry rose with undiminished clamor. The English pushed forward amid the pitchy darkness. At every pause they made, the retiring enemy would gather to renew the attack, firing back hotly upon the front and flanks. To advance further would be useless, and the only alternative was to withdraw and wait for daylight. This task was commenced amid a sharp fire from both sides; and before it was completed, heavy volleys were heard from the rear, where Captain Grant was stationed. It was now evident that instant retreat was necessary; and the command being issued to that effect, the men fell back into marching order, and slowly began their retrograde movement. Grant was now in the van, and Dalzell at the rear. They reached a point where, close upon the right, were many barns and out-houses, with strong picket fences. Behind these, and in a newly dug cellar close at hand, lay concealed a great multitude of Indians. They suffered the advanced party to pass unmolested, but when the center and rear came opposite their ambuscade, they raised a frightful yell, and poured a volley among them. The men had well-nigh fallen into a panic, and but for the presence of Dalzell, the retreat would have been turned into a flight. 'The enemy,' writes an officer who was in the fight, 'marked him for his extraordinary bravery;' and he had already received two severe wounds. Yet his exertions did not slacken for a moment. Some of the soldiers he rebuked, some he threatened, and some he beat with the flat of his sword.

"The enemy had taken possession of a house, from the windows of which they fired down upon the English. Major Rogers, with some of his provincial rangers, burst the door with an axe, rushed in, and expelled them, and now the fire of the Indians, being much diminished, the retreat was resumed. No sooner had the men faced about, than the savages came darting through the mist upon their flank and rear, cutting down stragglers, and scalping the fallen. At a little distance lay a sergeant of the 55th, helplessly wounded; raising himself on his hands, and gazing with a look of despair after his retiring comrades. The sight caught the eye of Dalzell. That gallant soldier, in the true spirit of heroism, ran out amid the firing to rescue the wounded man, when a shot struck him, and he fell dead.

"In the meantime, Captain Grant, with his advanced party, had moved forward about half a mile, where he found some orchards and inclosures, by means of which he could maintain himself until the center and rear should arrive. From this point he detached all the men he could spare to occupy the houses below; and as soldiers soon began to come in from the rear, he was enabled to re-enforce these detachments, until a complete line of communication was established with the fort, and the retreat effectually secured. Within an hour the whole party had arrived, with the exception of Rogers and his men, who were quite unable to come off, being besieged in the house of Campan by full two hundred Indians. The two armed bateaux had gone down to the fort, laden with the dead and wounded. They now returned, and in obedience to an order from Grant, proceeded up the river to a point opposite Campan's house, where they opened a fire of swivels, which swept the ground above and below it, and completely scattered the assailants. Rogers and his party now came out, and marched down the road to unite themselves with Grant. The two bateaux accompanied them closely, and, by a constant fire, restrained the Indians from making an attack.

"About eight o'clock, after six hours of marching and combat, the detachment entered once more within the sheltering palisades of Detroit.

"The Indians were greatly elated by their success. Runners were sent out for several hundred miles through the surrounding woods, to spread tidings of the victory; and re-enforcements soon began to come in to swell the force of Pontiac. 'Fresh warriors,' writes Gladwyn, 'arrive almost every day, and I believe that I shall soon be besieged by upwards of a thousand.' But nothing worthy of notice occurred, until the night of the 4th of September.

"The schooner *Gladwyn*, the smaller of the two armed vessels so often mentioned, had been sent down to Niagara with letters and dispatches. She was now returning. The night set in with darkness so complete that at the distance of a few rods nothing could be discerned. Meantime, three hundred and fifty Indians, in their birch canoes, glided silently down with the current, and were close upon the vessel before they were seen. There was only time to fire a single cannon-shot among them before they were beneath her bows and clambering up her sides, holding their knives clinched fast between their teeth The crew gave them a close fire of musketry, without any effect; then, flinging down their guns, they seized the spears and hatchets with which they were all provided, and met the assailants with such furious energy and courage that in the space of two or three minutes they had killed and wounded more than twice their own number. But the Indians were only checked for a moment. The master of the vessel was killed, several of the crew were disabled, and the assailants were leaping over the bulwarks, when Jacobs, the mate, called out to blow up the schooner. This desperate command saved her and her crew. Some Wyandots, who had gained the deck, caught the meaning of his words, and gave the alarm to their companions. Instantly every Indian leaped overboard in a panic, and the whole were seen diving and swimming off in all directions, to escape the threatened explosion. The schooner was cleared of her assailants, who did not dare to renew the attack; and on the following morning she sailed for the fort, which she reached without molestation."

From Dunmore's War, through the French and English contest, through the Revolution, through the surrender of the lake forts by the English, through St. Clair's disastrous defeat, through the joy of "Mad Anthony" Wayne's victory and the glory of the Thames and Tippecanoe, down to the final pacification of the border by General William Henry Harrison, the "Pioneers of the West" were in the fore-front of battle. From first to last the older records best tell the story.

"The battle of Point Pleasant took place in Dunmore's War, October 10, 1774. It was the bloodiest battle perhaps ever fought with the Indians in Virginia. It had its origin in a variety of causes; but that which more than all others hastened the crisis was the murder of the family of Logan by the whites, at or near the mouth of Yellow Creek. This disgraceful act is, by some, imputed to Colonel Cresap, a distinguished frontiersman, who resided near the town of Wheeling. Logan at least believed him to be the guilty party. By others it is strongly denied that Colonel Cresap was a participant in the affair. But, be this as it may, the act, in addition to other exasperations, had greatly incensed the Indian tribes on the north of the Ohio River.

"To protect the settlements bordering on the Upper Ohio, it soon became necessary to organize an army in the East sufficient to operate against the savages.

"The army destined for the expedition was composed of volunteers and militia, chiefly from the counties west of the Blue Ridge, and consisted of two divisions. The Northern Division, comprehending the troops collected in Frederick, Dunmore (now Shenandoah), and the adjacent counties, was to be commanded by Lord Dunmore in person; and the Southern, comprising the different companies raised in Bottetourt, Augusta, and the adjoining counties east of the Blue Ridge, was to be led on by General Andrew Lewis. These two divisions, proceeding by different routes, were to form a junction at the mouth of the Big Kanawha, and from thence penetrate the country north-west of the Ohio River, as far as the season would permit, and destroy all the Indian towns and villages they could reach.

"When the Southern Division arrived at Point Pleasant, Governor Dunmore, with the forces under his command, had not reached there; however, advices were received from his lordship that he had determined on proceeding across the country directly to the Shawnee towns,* and

---

*On the Scioto River, about eighty miles north-west of Point Pleasant.

INDIAN CONFLICTS.   137

ordering General Lewis to cross the river, march forward and form a junction with him near to them. These advices were received on the 9th of October, and preparations were immediately commenced for the transportation of the troops over the Ohio River.

"Early on the morning of Monday, the 10th of that month, two soldiers left the camp and proceeded up the Ohio River in quest of deer. When they progressed about two miles, they unexpectedly came in sight of a large number of Indians rising from their encampment, and who, discovering the hunters, fired upon them and killed one; the other escaped unhurt, and, running briskly to the camp, communicated the intelligence 'that he had seen a body of the enemy covering four acres of ground as closely as they could stand by the side of each other.' The main part of the army was immediately ordered out under Colonel Lewis and William Fleming, and, having formed into two lines, they proceeded about four hundred yards, when they met the Indians, and the action commenced.

"At the first onset, Colonel Charles Lewis having fallen, and Colonel Fleming being wounded, both lines gave way, and were retreating briskly toward the camp, when they were met by a re-enforcement under Colonel Field, and rallied. The engagement then became general, and was sustained by the most obstinate fury on both sides. The Indians, perceiving that the 'tug of war' had come, and determined on affording the Colonial army no chance of escape if victory should declare for them, formed a line extending across the point from the Ohio to the Kanawha, and protected in front by logs and fallen timber. In this situation they maintained the contest with unabated vigor from sunrise till toward the close of evening, bravely and successfully resisting every charge which was made on them, and withstanding the impetuosity of every onset with the most invincible firmness, until a fortunate movement on the part of the Virginian troops decided the day.

"Some short distance above the entrance of the Kanawha River into the Ohio there is a stream called Crooked Creek, emptying into the former of these from the north-east, whose banks are tolerably high, and were then covered with a thick and luxuriant growth of weeds. Seeing the impracticability of dislodging the Indians by the most vigorous attack, and sensible of the great danger which must arise to his army if the contest were not decided before night, General Lewis detached the three companies which were commanded by Captains Isaac Shelby, George Matthews, and John Stewart, with orders to proceed up the Kanawha River and Crooked Creek, under cover of the banks and weeds, till they could pass some distance beyond the enemy, when they were to emerge from their covert, march downward toward the point, and attack the Indians in the rear. The maneuver thus planned was promptly executed, and gave a decided victory to the Colonial army. The Indians, finding themselves suddenly and unexpectedly encompassed between two armies, and not doubting but in the rear was the looked-for re-enforcement under Colonel Christian, soon gave way, and about sundown commenced a precipitate retreat across the Ohio to the towns on the Scioto.

"The victory indeed was decisive, and many advantages were obtained by it, but they were not cheaply bought. The Virginian army sustained in this engagement a loss of seventy-five killed and one hundred and forty wounded, about one-fifth of the entire number of troops.

"Nor could the number of the enemy engaged be ever ascertained. Their army is known to have been made up of warriors from the different nations north of the Ohio, and to have comprised the flower of the tribes already mentioned. The distinguished chief and consummate warrior, Cornstalk, who commanded their forces, proved himself on that day to be justly entitled to the prominent station which he occupied. His plan of alternate retreat and attack was well conceived, and occasioned the principal loss sustained by the whites. If at any time his warriors were believed to waver, his voice could be heard above the din of arms, exclaiming in his native tongue: 'Be strong! Be strong!' And when one near him, by trepidation and reluctance to proceed to the charge, evinced a dastardly disposition, fearing the example might have a pernicious influence, with one blow of the tomahawk he severed his skull. It was perhaps a solitary instance in which terror predominated. Never did men exhibit a more conclusive evidence of bravery in making a charge, and fortitude in withstanding an onset, than did those undisciplined soldiers of the forest in the field at Point Pleasant.

"Having buried the dead, and made every arrangement of which their situation admitted for the comfort of the wounded, intrenchments were thrown up, and the army commenced its march to form a junction with the northern division under Lord Dunmore. Proceeding by the way of the Salt Licks General Lewis pressed forward with astonishing rapidity (considering that the march was through a trackless desert); but before he had gone far an express arrived from Dunmore with orders to return immediately to the mouth of the Big Kanawha. Suspecting the integrity of his lordship's motives, and urged by the advice of his officers generally, General Lewis refused to obey these orders, and continued to advance till he was met at Kilkenny Creek,* and in sight of an Indian village which its inhabitants had just fired and deserted, by the governor, accompanied by White Eyes, who informed him that he was negotiating a treaty of peace, which would supersede the necessity of any further movement of the Southern Division, and repeated the order for his return.

"On his arrival at Point Pleasant, General Lewis left a sufficient force to protect the place, and a supply of provisions for the wounded, and then led the balance of the division to the place of rendezvous (Lewisburg) and disbanded them."

Into this story of Dunmore's War comes a sadder page; for it emphasizes a history which runs through more than one "Century of Dishonor!"—the history of the Indians' wrongs and the Government's shame:

"Cornstalk had, from the first, opposed the war with the whites, and when his scouts reported the advance of General Lewis's division the sagacious chief did all he could to restrain his men and keep them from battle. But all his remonstrances were in vain, and it was *then* he told them, 'As you are determined to fight, you *shall* fight.' After their defeat and return home, a council was convened to determine upon what was next to be done. The stern old chief said, rising: 'What shall we do now? The Long Knives are coming upon us by two routes. Shall we turn out and fight them? Shall we kill all our squaws and children, and then fight until we are killed ourselves?' Still the congregated warriors were silent, and, after a moment's hesitation, Cornstalk struck his tomahawk into the war-post, and with compressed lips and flashing eyes gazed around the assembled group; then, with great emphasis, spoke: 'Since you are not inclined to fight I will go and make peace.'

"Lord Dunmore, on his return to Camp Charlotte, concluded a treaty

---

* Congo, a branch of the Scioto.

with the Indians. Cornstalk was the chief speaker on the part of the Indians. He openly charged the whites with being the sole cause of the war, enumerating the many provocations which the Indians had received, and dwelling with great force and emphasis upon the diabolical murder of Logan's family. This great chief spoke in the most vehement and denunciatory style. His loud, clear voice was distinctly heard throughout the camp.

"But there was one who would not attend the camp of Lord Dunmore, and that was Logan. The Mingo chief felt the chill of despair at his heart; his very soul seemed frozen within him; and, although he would not interpose obstacles to an amicable adjustment of existing difficulties, still he could not meet the Long Knives in council as if no terrible stain of blood rested upon their hands. He remained at a distance, brooding in melancholy silence over his accumulated wrongs during most of the time his friends were negotiating. But Dunmore felt the importance of at least securing his assent, and for that purpose sent a special messenger, Colonel John Gibson, who waited upon the chief at his wigwam. The messenger in due time returned, bringing with him the celebrated speech which has given its author an immortality almost as imperishable as that of the great Athenian orator. The speech was probably prepared by Colonel John Gibson, and polished either by himself or some one else skilled in the art of composition. Its authorship has been ascribed to Mr. Jefferson. But after reading the highly eulogistic terms in which that gentleman speaks of it, one could hardly suppose it to have been written by him. He says: 'I may challenge the whole orations of Demosthenes and Cicero, and of any more eminent orator (if Europe has furnished a more eminent), to produce a single passage superior to it.' This would be rather too much for any modest writer to say of his own performance. It may be added, that De Witt Clinton indorsed the opinion expressed by Mr. Jefferson as to this celebrated speech.

"But that the intelligent reader may judge for himself, the speech of Logan, as found in Jefferson's Notes, is given here:

"'I appeal,' says he, 'to any white man to say, if he ever entered Logan's cabin hungry, and he gave him not meat; if he ever came cold and naked, and he clothed him not. During the course of the last long and bloody war, Logan remained idle in his cabin and advocated peace. Such was my love for the whites, that my countrymen pointed as they passed and said, "Logan is the friend of the white man." I had even thought to live with you but for the injuries of one man. Colonel Cresap, the last Spring, in cold blood and unprovoked, murdered all the relations of Logan, not even sparing my women and children. There runs not a drop of my blood in the veins of any living creature. This called on me for revenge. I have sought it; I have killed many; I have fully glutted my vengeance. For my country, I rejoice at the beams of peace, but do not harbor the thought that mine is the joy of fear. Logan never felt fear. He will not turn on his heel to save his life. Who is there to mourn for Logan? Not one.'

"In the year 1777 the Indians, being urged by British agents, became very troublesome to the frontier settlements, manifesting much appearance of hostility, when Cornstalk, with Redhawk, paid a visit to the garrison at Point Pleasant. He made no secret of the disposition of the Indians, declaring that on his part he was opposed to joining in the war on the side of the British, but that all the nations except himself and his own tribe were determined to engage in it, and that of course he and his tribe would have to run with the stream.

"On this Captain Arbuckle thought proper to detain him, Redhawk, and another fellow as hostages, to prevent the nation from joining the British.

"During our stay two young men by the names of Hamilton and Gilmore went over the Kanawha one day to hunt for deer. On their return to camp, some Indians had concealed themselves on the bank, among some weeds, to view our encampment, and as Gilmore came along past them, they fired on him and killed him on the bank.

"'Captain Arbuckle and myself were standing on the opposite bank when the gun fired, and while we were considering who it could be shooting contrary to orders, or what they were doing over the river, we saw Hamilton run down the bank, who called out that Gilmore was killed. Gilmore was one of the company of Captain John Hall, of that part of the country now Rockbridge County. The captain was a relation of Gilmore, whose family and friends were nearly all killed by the Indians in the year 1763, when Greenbrier was cut off. Hall's men instantly jumped into a canoe and went to the relief of Hamilton, who was standing in momentary expectation of being put to death. They brought the corpse of Gilmore down the bank, covered with blood and scalped, and put him into the canoe.

As they were passing the river, I observed to Captain Arbuckle that the people would be for killing the hostages as soon as the canoe should land. He supposed they would not offer to commit so great a violence upon the innocent, who were in no wise accessory to the murder of Gilmore. But the canoe had hardly touched the shore until the cry was raised, "Let us kill the Indians in the fort," and every man, with gun in hand, came up the bank, full of rage. Captain Hall was at their head and led them. Captain Arbuckle and I met them, and endeavored to dissuade them from so unjustifiable an action; but they cocked their guns, threatened us with instant death if we did not desist, rushed by us into the fort, and put the Indians to death.

"'On the preceding day, Cornstalk's son, Elinipsico, had come from the nation to see his father, and to know if he was well or alive. When he came to the river opposite the fort he hallooed. His father was at that instant in the act of delineating, at our request, with chalk on the floor, a map of the country and the waters between the Shawanese towns and the Mississippi. He immediately recognized the voice of his son, got up, went out, and answered him. The young fellow crossed over, and they embraced each other in the most tender and affectionate manner. As the men advanced to the door Cornstalk rose up and met them. They fired upon him, and seven or eight bullets went through him. So fell Cornstalk, the great warrior, whose name was bestowed upon him by the consent of the nation as their great strength and support. His son was shot dead as he sat upon a stool. Redhawk made an attempt to go up the chimney; but was shot down. The other Indian was shamefully mangled, and I grieved to see him so long in the agonies of death.

"The murder of Cornstalk and his party of course produced its natural effect, deciding the wavering Shawanese to join the other tribes as allies of the British, and converting them from possible friends of the American cause into the most bitter and relentless enemies."

During the entire period of the Revolutionary War there was an almost constant succession of daring raids and desperate encounters upon the Western frontier.

Furnished with English weapons, and occasionally led by British officers, the Indians made constant inroads into Kentucky and Western Virginia; and hardly one of the scattered settlements south of the OHIO RIVER escaped without severe loss, even when its defenders succeeded in beating back their assailants. A death of torture, or a captivity which beggars description, awaited the hapless prisoners, taken from their fancied security in the distant regions far back of the line of blockhouses and stations. In fact, there was no assurance or hope of safety for the women and children, except the shelter of the little log forts, which were defended by the rifles of the matchless marksmen of the border.

The most life-like sketches of the time which we have been able to glean from the early chronicles, have already been presented to the reader in brief extracts from the traditions and records of the "Early Settlements." Nearly all of these sketches belong to the sparsely inhabited era; yet we must not lose sight of the fact that the increase and growth of these settlements brought a fuller life into the wilderness.

In Kentucky, Western Virginia, and Pennsylvania "blockhouses" were still in existence during the last decade of the eighteenth century, but around each a village had grown. The forests between the "stations" were cut by wide swaths of clearings; homely little cabins were nestled at the base of the linked chain of the beautiful rounded hills, which are the most distinctive characteristic of the valley of the Ohio; and the more pretentious log houses of the "proprietors" dotted the rich bottomlands of the south-eastern affluents of the RIVER.

The advent of this semi-civilization had changed and softened the savage features of the wilderness. The tangled solitudes were awakening into a new life. This rich wild nature— heretofore jealously guarding her hidden treasures—was now an open book to the SURVEYOR, who had followed hard upon the footsteps of the PIONEER.

Indian trails were enlarging into "new roads;" openings, where adventurous backwoodsmen had "cleared their lots," were closing up and coming together; and the regular weekly "mail-wagon" rattled across the "corduroy bridges," or changed horses at the log stable, under shady, overarching trees; where, within a past which could be counted by single numbers, the express-rider had ridden in hot haste to distance a bullet or pass an ambuscade before the deadly tomahawk could disable his horse or strike him from his seat.

From the villages, where the houses clustered together for good neighborship as well as for defense, the "clearings" began to stretch out over the swelling ridges, exhibiting their summer's wealth in wide, billowy waves of yellow corn and green pastures; and on the sunny southern slopes peach and apple orchards marked the coming of spring, with their delicate sweet blossoms. The bronze-crested, flame-throated, purple-winged humming-bird, leaving his Winter home by the Gulf, came up the river when he knew the wild honeysuckles would be in bloom; but the orchard scents caught him, and he forgot the pretty wild things in the glen, and hung in mid-air above the lovely buds, in the rapt delight of a new joy. All the twittering little feathered creatures, that care for man and seek his companionship, came flocking into the open glades that edged the deeper forests; for the *Dark and Bloody Ground* was losing its somber shades, and its haunted forest-aisles were no longer the hiding-places of the death-dealing red men. The fiat had gone forth; the land-loving Saxon and his affiliated Celtic brother had won, and would hold, the south bank of "The White Shining River," which the tribes

SPANNING NORTH FORK.

were never more to see. In their visions of the happy hunting-grounds there would be a reproduction of its banks; or at least a dream-given likeness in those far-away shining shores of peace.

On the north bank the contest was about to begin on a larger scale. War was to be war. Squadrons of horsemen, companies of infantry, troops marching with banners, were now about to drive the Indians to that uncertain NORTH-WEST which is always changing its boundaries. From the beginning of time, as time is counted by struggles and battles, the Indians were always on the losing side. As allies of the French they were conquered by the English; as allies of the English they fought through the Revolution, and for years after the surrender of Cornwallis kept the war spirit, which is the spirit of hell, alive upon the border. The fire of hatred between the borderer and the Indian was unextinguishable. At every breath of rumour hostilities broke out afresh. Foot by foot the Eastern tribes had been driven to the Alleghanies, across the chain, into the fertile belts and magnificent forests of the loveliest of lovely river valleys. There they would have rested, and for that they joined the confederacy of the Miamis. But the Saxon followed hard and fast. Their new allies in the West were to suffer defeat and loss, and the broad free lands of all the nations, watered by the most beautiful of the tributaries of the RIVER which was their pride and their delight, were to be the spoil of the conquerors.

Every defeat compelled the tribes to go backward. Every treaty of peace was an enforced sale of the lands upon which they collected the peltries that brought them comparatively nothing, but that made the gains of the white trader.

Their removal from the Ohio had now come to be a question of life and death to the tribes upon the Ohio; for year by year they were steadily nearing the Mississippi, and near by the Mississippi were their un-friends, the Illinois, and across the Mississippi their deadly enemies, the Sioux. The wisest of their chiefs, their prophets, foretold their utter destruction, and the warriors understood that the final day of resistance had come. The tomahawk, the scalping-knife, the rifle, and their most desperate powers of endurance and resistance, must decide their ownership of any lands east of the Mississippi; for if they made friends with the Illinois, and found favor with the haughty, imperious Sioux, who could assure them that the persistent "Long Knives" would not cross the mighty waters? All through the century they had been fighting the same foe—the same Virginia and Pennsylvania pioneers—the men who preferred the hunting, the rude sports, and the desperate frays of the border to the ways of peace.

Back of the "Long Knives" a different, yet a no less persistent and inimical people, were following in their wake. The New Englander had heard of the fertile valleys; of the land flowing, if not "with milk and honey," with the traffic that breeds riches. He was as godly a sectarist as could be found in the fighting Scotch-Irish stock; and though a less picturesque figure than the sturdy pioneer, he had come to stay. *This* new-comer felt it to be part of the eternal fitness of things, for the rough fellow in the hunting-shirt and the buckskin breeches to go onward, while he rested upon the rich lands which bordered the broad-bosomed river.

The 1st of March, 1784, Virginia ceded her North-west Territory to the United States, to be laid out and formed into States, "having the same rights of sovereignty, freedom, and independence as the other States." Among other conditions,

INDIAN CONFLICTS. 147

"they were to be FREE STATES," and all "French Canadians, and other settlers," were to "hold their possessions in peace." The VIRGINIA OHIO COMPANY had builded forts, and assisted with material aid the men who fought the Indians and the English through the dark days of the Colonies and the sufferings of the Revolution; fought every step of the road of conquest, from the topmost ridge of the Alleghanies to the Falls of the Ohio, until the fight for the river was won. The next work to be done—work in which all must assist, for the newly arrived settler on the north bank must be protected—was the *pacification* or the *extermination* of the Miamis and their new allies.

Pontiac was dead. Little Turtle was as yet an unknown quantity among the chiefs. The government was about to build defensive works, to be commanded and held by regulars, and a fair contingent of armed troops were to be assembled within striking distance of the malcontents, who "were sulking in their villages." This was the situation in the last decade of the eighteenth century.

The gallant but unfortunate, or incapable (a question never settled conclusively) St. Clair, had been appointed by Washington GOVERNOR OF THE NORTH-WEST TERRITORY. His headquarters were at Marietta, at the mouth of the Muskingum— one of the several towns founded the same year in which Losantiville (Cincinnati) was laid out. The following extracts, collected and condensed from the "St. Clair Papers," are probably fairer in expression than the almost universal condemnation of his contemporaries, and for that reason will best tell the story of the defeat, which ended in a disgraceful rout:

"Receiving from Major Hamtramck the information that Antoine Gamelin had failed to persuade the Wabash Indians to enter into a treaty

Governor St. Clair hastened to complete the work of organization. Before his departure for Philadelphia, he wrote to Major Hamtramck, advising him of his purpose to prepare for a military movement against the Indians on the Wabash, and that Colonel Sargent would proceed to Post Vincennes, to make the civil appointments and organize the militia. The report of Mr. Gamelin is of extraordinary interest. It shows that the machinations of Brant and his British friends had been successful, that the Indians proposed to fight, and expected to force the Americans back across the Ohio.

"General St. Clair, after conferring with General Harmar, determined to send an expedition against the Maumee towns, under the command of that officer. A circular letter was issued to the county lieutenants of Kentucky and Western Pennsylvania, informing them that there was no prospect of a peace with the tribes on the Wabash, and instructing them to call out the militia allotted to their respective counties, to meet at Fort Washington by the 15th of September.

"When the militia did arrive, General Harmar was much disheartened, as they were 'raw, and unused to the gun or woods.' In addition, a large portion of the arms were unfit for use, many of the muskets and rifles being without locks. The militia officers quarreled, and the men were insubordinate. Colonel Hardin was the senior officer, yet some of the men declared they would return home unless another officer could lead them, and a compromise became necessary.

"When on the march, October 2d, the force was reviewed, it was found to consist of three hundred and twenty regulars, under the immediate command of Majors Wyllys and Doughty, and one thousand one hundred and thirty-three militia, under the command of Colonel Hardin, an old Continental officer. The route was by old Chillicothe, at the headwaters of the LittleMiami; thence to Mad River, and thence to the Miami, which they struck near the ruins of the old trading-post.

"Here they captured a Shawanese Indian, who informed them that the Indians were leaving their village (distant about thirty miles), as fast as possible. Colonel Hardin was detached with six hundred light troops and one company of regulars. He was instructed to push for the Miami village, which was at the junction of the St. Joseph and St. Mary Rivers, and take every precaution to keep his men under strict discipline. When he reached the village, on the 15th, he found it deserted. On the 17th he was joined by the main body, and the order was given for the destruction of the buildings, and the vast fields of corn stretching along the bottoms of the streams.

"On the following day Colonel Trotter was ordered out with three hundred militia and thirty regulars, under Captain Armstrong, with instructions to see if he could find traces of the Indians. He returned at night without having accomplished any thing. The next day Colonel Hardin went out with the same command. Before he had proceeded very far many of the militia deserted. When distant from camp ten miles, he suddenly came upon about one hundred Indians, and was entirely defeated. At the moment of attack by the Indians, the remainder of the militia fled, without firing a shot. The regulars stood firm, and suffered severely.

"On the 21st, the army—having burned the chief town and five of the Indian villages, and destroyed twenty thousand bushels of corn in the ear, the object of the expedition—took up their line of march back to Fort Washington, and encamped eight miles from the ruins. At nine o'clock, at the solicitation of Colonel Hardin, General Harmar ordered out four hundred men, including sixty regulars, under Major Wyllys, with instructions to go back to the Indian town on the head-waters of the Miami, to surprise any parties that might have returned there. The militia came upon a few Indians immediately after crossing the river, put them to flight, and, contrary to orders, the pursuit was continued up the St. Joseph for several miles. The center, composed of the regular troops, was soon afterwards attacked by the main body of the Indians, under Little Turtle, and although they fought with desperation, were obliged to give way. The few survivors fled in the direction taken by the militia, and met them returning from the pursuit of the scattering Indians. They were followed by the Indians, who attempted to pass the stream, but were repulsed. The troops, after collecting the wounded, returned to camp. The regulars lost two officers, Major Wyllys and Lieutenant Frothingham.

"The result of St. Clair's visit to Philadelphia, and his report on affairs in the territory, was: First, to send a formidable military force into the Miami country to erect a series of forts, as recommended by him the preceding year; and secondly, to send minor expeditions against the Wabash tribes to punish them for their marauding in the spring of 1790. A new regiment was to be added to the military force, and General St. Clair was to conduct the expedition against the Miami towns in person, with General Richard Butler second in command. The equipment was to be complete in all respects, and the most cordial co-operation was promised by the War Department.

"The following entry is found in Major Denny's journal, under the date of September 1st: 'General St. Clair appears exceeding impatient at the delay or detention of some of the corps.'

"It was the 7th of September before General Butler and Quartermaster-General Hodgden arrived at Fort Washington. St. Clair had already moved forward his two thousand men—*not* three thousand effectives, as promised by the Secretary of War—about twenty-four miles. Forts Hamilton and Jefferson were constructed under the greatest difficulties, as the rainy season had set in.

"The 24th of October the little army left Fort Jefferson, and moved through the wilderness towards the Maumee, where another fort was to be erected. The frost had cut off the forage, the men were on half rations, and the militia deserted in such numbers that the general found it necessary to dispatch Major Hamtramck with the First Regiment, three hundred strong, to arrest them and bring up the provisions that were supposed to be *en route*.

"Every precaution was taken on the march and in camp to guard against a surprise. On the 3d of November, 1791, the troops encamped on high ground on a small creek, supposed to be a branch of the Maumee, but which was, in fact, a branch of the Wabash. The high ground was barely sufficient for the regulars in rather contracted lines. The militia, under Colonel Oldham, passed beyond the creek a quarter of a mile, and encamped in parallel lines. Before midnight General Butler dispatched Captain Slough, with thirty-two men, to reconnoiter in front of the lines. He saw enough Indians to confirm the opinion that the troops would be attacked in the morning. He immediately returned to camp and communicated to General Butler what he had learned, and added that, if thought proper, he would make the report to General St. Clair. General Butler remained silent for some time, and then remarked that he 'must feel fatigued, and he had better go and lie down.' Captain Slough obeyed.

"General Butler neither communicated to General St. Clair the information, nor took any further precaution against the enemy. On the morning of the 4th, a half hour before sunrise, an attack was made on the militia. The militia fled pell-mell through the first line of regulars, who were attempting to form. However, the enemy was well received by the front line; but almost instantly the entire camp seemed to be surrounded by an unseen foe.

"The men were pressed toward the center, and fell by scores under the unerring aim of the savages, who fired from the woody covert surrounding them.

"General St. Clair, who had left his sick quarters upon the first fire, repeatedly directed the men to charge against the skulking foe, who fled before the bayonet, and then returned to the attack.

"The uniforms of the officers attracted the aim of the savages, and they fell on every hand. Among those wounded early in the engagement was General Butler, but he continued to urge resistance. When, at last, all of the artillery officers had been either killed or wounded, and the fire of the Indians was so near and deadly as to threaten the annihilation of the force, preparation was made for a retreat.

"A last charge was made against the enemy, and a retreat accomplished. 'At the moment of the retreat,' says Major Denny, 'one of the few horses saved had been procured for the general; he was on foot until then; I kept by him, and he delayed to see the rear come up.' The general then commanded Major Denny to 'push to the front and rally a force sufficient to check the panic.' Then he turned his attention to the care of those who were partially disabled by wounds. As he and the officer in command of the rear-guard moved over the route, evidence was seen on every hand that the retreat had been a disgraceful flight, even to the very gates of Fort Jefferson, where, at last, under the assuring presence of Major Hamtramck's regulars, terror gave place to confidence.

"The killed and missing officers numbered thirty-seven, and the privates five hundred and ninety-three; the wounded, thirty-one officers, and two hundred and fifty-two privates. Not an officer exposed himself as much as the general, and yet it was always with a calm courage, seeking to reach the enemy effectively. 'I have nothing to lay to the charge of the troops,' said he in his official report, 'but their want of discipline, which from the short time they had been in service, it was impossible they should have acquired, and which rendered it very difficult, when they were thrown into confusion, to reduce them again to order, and this is one reason why the loss has fallen so heavy on the officers, who did every thing in their power to re-form the troops.'

"It seems surprising, in reviewing the evidence of so many witnesses, that the commanding general, who was believed to be competent, whose courage had been often proved, who knew the superiority of the Indian forces—warriors trained to war from infancy—should think of hazarding, with such disorderly troops, and under such circumstances, his reputation and life, and the lives of others.

"St. Clair asked to have an inquiry made by military officers, but that being impracticable, the matter came before Congress, and was there thoroughly examined.

"After his return to Fort Washington, on the 9th of November, St. Clair wrote his official dispatch to the Secretary of War, which contained a comprehensive account of the disastrous campaign. There is no fault-finding, no allusion to the shameful mismanagement in the War Department, and nothing as to the neglect of Colonel Oldham and General Butler to advise him of the presence of the enemy on the night of the 3d of November. Major Denny was charged with its prompt delivery, and arriving in Philadelphia at a late hour on the 19th, he waited immediately upon the Secretary of War and delivered the dispatches.

"The President declared that General St. Clair should have justice.

"'More satisfactory testimony in favor of St. Clair is furnished by the circumstance that he still retained the undiminished esteem and good opinion of Washington.' This we read in the work of Chief-Justice Marshall. St. Clair resigned his conmission in the army, and General Anthony Wayne was appointed to succeed him in April, 1792.

"The whole country had been thrown into consternation and mourning by the news of the defeat of St. Clair. A succession of disasters to the American arms had rendered the Indian war, to the last degree, unpopular; and no little of the odium attached itself to the Administration under whose auspices it had been conducted. Parties had already developed themselves in Congress and the nation, and the conduct of the Indian war furnished abundant ground for the ill-disposed to raise charges against, and excite distrust of, the wisdom of the Administration.

"Thus situated, to sustain the honor of the government, to vindicate the superiority of the American arms, to arrest the clamor of party, to give protection to the frontier settlements, and, if possible, to restore a safe and lasting peace with the Indian Nations, new measures were to be adopted.

"The highest exercise of the wisdom of Washington, in the selection of a commander-in-chief for the army, was demanded; for on this selection, more than on any which had been made since the commencement of the Revolutionary War, every thing dear to the country depended. Having acted with Wayne in the most trying scenes of the Revolutionary War, the President had a thorough knowledge of his fitness for the important command.

"On the 25th of May, 1792, Wayne having been furnished, by the Secretary of War, with the instructions of the President, in which it was emphatically expressed 'that another defeat would be inexpressibly ruinous to the reputation of the government,' immediately took leave of his family and friends, and repaired to Pittsburgh, the place appointed for the rendezvous of the troops, where he arrived early in June.

"General Wayne did not permit the summer to pass without adopting proper measures to ascertain the strength and disposition of the hostile Indians. Efforts were made to impress on their minds the earnest desire of the American government to make peace on terms that should be mutually just and honorable, and yet to leave no doubt that, if war was preferred by them, they would contend with a different force from that which they had previously encountered. Colonel Harding and Major Trueman were sent with flags of truce to the Indians, but they were both wantonly murdered.

"In the meantime the Indians continued their raids upon the frontier, except in the immediate neighborhood of posts occupied by detachments of troops, and many valuable lives were lost.

"Suitable winter quarters having been selected by Wayne, the army left Pittsburgh on the 28th of November, and took up a position on the Ohio, twenty-two miles below that place, and seven above the mouth of the Big Beaver, to which he gave the name of Legionville. Here the troops were hutted, the camp was fortified, and every possible preparation for defense adopted.

"Anxious to conciliate the Six Nations of Indians, Wayne sent an invitation to two distinguished chiefs, Cornplanter and New Arrow, to visit him at Legionville, at which place they arrived in March, 1793. A toast was given by Cornplanter, at the general's table, which will show the terms on which they wished peace. 'MY MIND AND HEART ARE UPON THAT RIVER,' said Cornplanter, pointing to the Ohio; 'MAY THAT WATER EVER CONTINUE TO RUN AND REMAIN THE BOUNDARY OF LASTING PEACE BETWEEN THE AMERICANS AND INDIANS ON ITS OPPOSITE SHORES!' Such was the boundary-line fixed upon by friendly Indians.

"The winter was not productive of any striking events; but early in April Wayne announced his readiness to descend the river, having a respectable body of well-disciplined troops, in whom he expressed perfect confidence, and the 30th of April, 1793, he left the camp at Legionville. The immediate destination of the troops was Fort Washington, then near the village, now the city, of Cincinnati. In six days the army arrived at the fort; but Wayne preferred a position a mile below, and named the new camp 'Hobson's Choice.' There the troops were disciplined, and arrangements were adopted for bringing into service an auxiliary aid of mounted volunteers from Kentucky.

"Intimations having been given by the Indians of a disposition to treat, a commission was appointed to meet them. As had been foreseen by Wayne, the negotiation failed. The Indians haughtily and peremptorily insisting 'THAT THE OHIO BE ESTABLISHED AS THE BOUNDARY, ON WHICH TERMS ALONE THEY WOULD CONDESCEND TO GRANT PEACE TO THE UNITED STATES.' But one course was left.

"General Wayne now took the most prompt measures to advance into the Indian country. On the 7th of October the army marched from 'Hobson's Choice,' and on the 13th took up a position six miles in advance of Fort Jefferson, on the south-west branch of the Miami. Wayne gave it the name of Greeneville, as a mark of respect to his Revolutionary friend, Major-General Greene. In a letter to the Secretary of War, dated from this camp, 23d October, 1793, the general gives an account of an attack on the 17th upon one of his convoys of provisions, under Lieutenant Lowrey and Ensign Boyd, consisting of ninety men. These two officers bravely fell after an obstinate resistance against superior numbers.

"In the meantime, General Scott, with a party of mounted men, arrived; but the season was too far advanced, and the force assembled was inadequate for decisive, active, operations, and they were permitted to return home.

"On December 23d General Wayne dispatched Major Burbeck, with eight companies of foot and a detachment of artillery, with orders to possess themselves of the field of St. Clair's defeat, November 4, 1791, and there to fortify. To this post was given the name of Fort Recovery. For the purpose of encouraging the troops who were ordered on this service, as well as for that of superintending the contemplated works, Wayne personally advanced to the same point, with a small re-enforcement of mounted infantry, accompanied by the officers mentioned in the following extract from general orders: 'The commander-in-chief returns his most grateful thanks to Major Henry Burbeck, and to every officer and private belonging to the detachment under his command, for their soldierly and exemplary good conduct during their late arduous tour of duty in repossessing General St. Clair's field of battle, and erecting thereon Fort Recovery.'

"More anxious to produce delay, and, perhaps, by their flags, to reconnoiter his position with safety than sincerely desirous of peace, the Indians, immediately after the erection of Fort Recovery, sent a pacific message to Wayne, and proposed that negotiations for a treaty should be opened, 'for the adjustment of all difficulties that existed.' Wayne, although he had no faith in their honesty of purpose, but regarded the proposal as a stratagem to further their hostile designs, did not feel himself warranted to decline the overture. He met their advance with a declaration of satisfaction; professed his entire readiness to make peace on terms that should be just; and only required, on their part, the release of the captives in their possession, as a proof of their sincerity. The flag departed, being allowed thirty days to return with the final answer of their chiefs.

"Upon the approach of spring, affairs assumed an aspect in the highest degree interesting, and called for the full exercise of the vigilance and wisdom of the commander of the army. Prompt measures were taken to garrison Fort Massac, thirty-eight miles above the mouth of the Ohio. The spoliations upon American commerce, and the hostile spirit of Great Britain, gave strong reasons to fear a war with that nation. Thus surrounded with difficulties and dangers, placed in circumstances which were as delicate as they were new and embarrassing, Wayne rose in proportion to the pressure, and showed that his abilities were equal to the emergency.

"In a letter from the Secretary of War, Wayne was authorized, should he deem it proper, to take the British fort on the rapids of the Miami. To the discretion of Wayne was therefore confided, not only the sole conduct of the Indian war, but the authority to take a step which must certainly have involved the nation in war with Great Britain. The time for active operations having come, and the Indians having failed to enter into negotiations for peace, Wayne called upon the governor of Kentucky for two thousand mounted volunteers.

"On the morning of the 30th of June an escort of ninety riflemen and fifty dragoons was attacked by a numerous body of Indians, under the walls of Fort Recovery, followed by a general assault upon that fort. The enemy, driven back by a deadly fire, renewed the attack with great spirit, but were finally repulsed with heavy loss. Circumstances, amounting nearly to positive proof, showed that the Indians were aided by a considerable auxiliary British force. Thus, on the very ground which was the scene of their proudest victory, the Indians were taught to respect the strength of American arms.

"It was past the middle of July before the mounted volunteers from Kentucky, under Major-General Scott, arrived at Greeneville. Every preparation which prudence could devise having been completed, Wayne moved with his main force, and but for the treachery and desertion of a soldier, the enemy would have suffered a complete surprise, when the troops arrived at Grand Glaize, in the very heart of the Indian settlements.

"Wayne entered the part of their settlement lying under the protection of the garrison of a British fort, a bold step, but prudent. 'Thus,' says Wayne in a letter to General Knox, 'we have gained possession of the grand emporium of the hostile Indians in the West without loss of blood.'

"He immediately erected a strong fortification at the confluence of the Auglaize and the Maumee, to which he gave the name 'Fort Defiance.' Though now prepared to strike the blow, the commander of the army, generous as brave, made one last effort to restore tranquillity without the further effusion of blood.

"Stimulated by their British allies, however, the Indians resolved to abide the issue of an engagement, and rejected the proposed offer.

"That engagement almost immediately followed, and a letter from Wayne to the Secretary of War described the engagement. From that letter the following extracts are taken:

"'It is with infinite pleasure that I now announce to you the brilliant success of the Federal army under my command. . . .

"'The enemy advanced from this place on the 15th, and arrived at

Roche de Bout on the 18th; the 19th we were employed in making a temporary post for the reception of our stores and baggage, and in reconnoitering the position of the enemy, who were encamped behind a thick, bushy wood and the British fort.

"'At eight o'clock on the morning of the 20th the army again advanced in columns, agreeably to the standing order of march. After advancing about five miles, Major Price's corps received so severe a fire from the enemy, who were secreted in the woods and high grass, as to compel them to retreat.

"'The legion was immediately formed in two lines, principally in a close, thick wood, which extended for miles on our left. . . .

"'I soon discovered, from the weight of the fire and extent of their lines, that the enemy were in full force in front, in possession of their favorite ground, and endeavoring to turn our left flank. I therefore gave orders for the second line to advance to support the first, and directed Major-General Scott to gain and turn the right flank of the savages, with the whole of the mounted volunteers, by a circuitous route; at the same time I ordered the front line to advance with trailed arms and rouse the Indians from their coverts at the point of the bayonet, and, when up, to deliver a close and well-directed fire on their backs, followed by a brisk charge, so as not to give time to load again.

"'All those orders were obeyed with spirit and promptitude; but such was the impetuosity of the charge by the first line of infantry, that the Indians and Canadian militia and volunteers were driven from all their coverts in so short a time that, although every exertion was used by the officers of the second legion, and by some of the mounted volunteers, to gain their proper positions, yet but a part of each could get up in season to participate in the action; the enemy being driven, in the course of one hour, more than two miles, through the thick woods already mentioned, by less than one-half their numbers.

"'The enemy amounted to two thousand combatants; the troops actually engaged against them were short of nine hundred. This horde of savages, with their allies, abandoned themselves to flight, and dispersed with terror and dismay, leaving our victorious army in full and quiet possession of the field of battle, which terminated within range of the guns of the British garrison. The loss of the enemy was more than double that of the Federal army.

"'We remained three days and nights on the banks of the Maumee, in front of the field of battle, during which time all the houses and corn-fields were consumed and destroyed for a considerable distance.

"'The army returned to this place on the 27th, laying waste the villages and corn-fields for fifty miles on each side of the Maumee. . . .

"'ANTHONY WAYNE.

"'*Dated, Grand Glaize, 28th August, 1794.*'

"In this decisive action the whole of Wayne's army in killed and wounded amounted only to one hundred and seven men. The loss of the enemy was more than double the number. The victory of the 20th of August, so glorious to the American arms, and the subsequent movement of the army, produced the most decisive effects. The lofty spirit of the Indians was broken, and the chiefs and warriors came forward and sued for peace."

Among the young soldiers who fought through their first campaign with "Mad Anthony" was a Virginian boy of twenty, whose gallantry won for him a place among the epauletted *aides*, and honorable mention in the order issued after the first battle. His people were "Colonial Virginians," his father had put his life in jeopardy by signing the Declaration of Independence. The boy was well born and well bred; but he carried the lightly filled purse which, of necessity, had to supply the wants of a younger son of a not over-rich country gentleman, whose estate had been taxed to provide for his servants and his family, while he faithfully filled the position of a delegate from Virginia in the Continental Congress.

In the olden-time generosity and hospitality were heavy taskmasters; and, when Benjamin Harrison of Berkeley died, all that could be done for his third son was to send him to his guardian in Philadelphia—Robert Morris, of Revolutionary memory—who placed him as a student of medicine with Dr. Benjamin Rush. The excitement on the frontier was so great that its echo dis-

"'We remained three days and nights on the banks of the Maumee, in front of the field of battle, during which time all the houses and corn-fields were consumed and destroyed for a considerable distance.

"'The army returned to this place on the 27th, laying waste the villages and corn-fields for fifty miles on each side of the Maumee. . . .

"'   ANTHONY WAYNE.

"'*Dated, Grand Glaize, 28th August, 1794.*'

"In this decisive action the whole of Wayne's army in killed and wounded amounted only to one hundred and seven men. The loss of the enemy was more than double the number. The victory of the 20th of August, so glorious to the American arms, and the subsequent movement of the army, produced the most decisive effects. The lofty spirit of the Indians was broken, and the chiefs and warriors came forward and sued for peace."

Among the young soldiers who fought through their first campaign with "Mad Anthony" was a Virginian boy of twenty, whose gallantry won for him a place among the epauletted *aides*, and honorable mention in the order issued after the first battle. His people were "Colonial Virginians," his father had put his life in jeopardy by signing the Declaration of Independence. The boy was well born and well bred; but he carried the lightly filled purse which, of necessity, had to supply the wants of a younger son of a not over-rich country gentleman, whose estate had been taxed to provide for his servants and his family, while he faithfully filled the position of a delegate from Virginia in the Continental Congress.

In the olden-time generosity and hospitality were heavy taskmasters; and, when Benjamin Harrison of Berkeley died, all that could be done for his third son was to send him to his guardian in Philadelphia—Robert Morris, of Revolutionary memory—who placed him as a student of medicine with Dr. Benjamin Rush. The excitement on the frontier was so great that its echo disturbed the calm repose of Philadelphia. The pulses of the placid "Friends" beat a trifle faster at the coming in of the daily stage which brought ominous news from the new settlements and the little army posts on the border.

The medical student's position was a thing of duty, not of choice; and now, from the stand-point of a born fighter, he began to see that it was altogether a more attractive career—and one that could placate duty with the plea of a greater need—to make wounds than to heal them. He reasoned with his guardian, with that impetuosity of youth which wins reason with the reasonableness of the thing it desires; and, besides, he pleaded the case with another old friend of his father's, who, caring for the service as well as for the boy, and having the power to serve his friend's son by serving the service, gave him an ensign's commission and sent him to Fort Washington to heat or cool his blood, according to the quality of his metal, with the sight of a routed army broken into fragments by a massacre unparalleled in the lesser horrors of all previous loss. Through sleet and snow the ensign's first march was back to the battle-ground of the dead, to bury the remains of the stricken—to gather the bloody harvest that cumbered the field of St. Clair's defeat.

In 1792 General Wayne was appointed to command the United States Legion, and young Harrison was promoted to a lieutenancy under that gallant soldier and rigid disciplinarian; who was attracted to the energetic, prompt, fearless, yet attentively obedient young subaltern. In a general order after the battle of the 23d December, General Wayne publicly thanked Lieutenant Harrison for his gallantry and good conduct. Again, in the fight with "the Little Turtle," August 20, 1794, when

Wayne won so signal a victory, Harrison was mentioned and *thanked* in the general orders. Upon the conclusion of the treaty with the Indians, Harrison was promoted to the rank of captain, and placed in command at Fort Washington.

At the death of General Wayne, in 1797, Captain Harrison left the army, and retired to his farm until he received his first civil appointment, that of secretary of the North-western Territory, and, *ex officio*, lieutenant-governor. His conduct in the office of secretary, and his sincerity and courteous manners, won him the confidence and good-will of all with whom he came in contact; and when, in the following year, the North-western Territory entered into the second grade of government, and the people were about to elect a delegate to Congress, he was the first representative chosen to fill that office. In the year 1800 the North-western Territory was divided. The part included within the present boundaries of Ohio and Michigan retained its new name, and the country to the north-west received the name of Indiana, the governorship of which was conferred by Jefferson on William Henry Harrison.

The powers intrusted to Harrison as governor of Indiana, and the extent of the territory confided to his jurisdiction, greater than had ever been heretofore committed to the charge of any citizen of the United States, except General Washington, burdened him with an immense responsibility. Indiana had then the boundaries of an empire, and to its governor almost unlimited power had been given. Ohio, having been cut out of the North-west Territory—ceded by Virginia to the United States— with definite boundaries, the remainder of the territory beyond the Ohio and Mississippi fell within his jurisdiction, including the wide regions that now compose the States north-west of the

THE CHERUB'S ROOST.

Ohio and east of the Mississippi; and, in fact, for a period of nearly two years the whole of Louisiana, which was attached to Indiana on its purchase in 1803, and was not erected into a separate territory until July, 1805.

The intermediate country was in possession of the Indians, and was visited by hunters, who were almost constantly embroiled with the savages. The tribes were restless and dissatisfied. Between the distant settlements the roads were the paths beaten by the Indians, and which were without ferries or even the rude bridges of the frontier. The seat of government was at Vincennes, a village beautifully situated on the Wabash, which was inhabited chiefly by the descendants of the French, who had built the town in the seventeenth century; and who, although attached to the new authority recently placed over them, were entirely unacquainted with our language and laws, and much preferred the simple institutions under which they had hitherto lived. Numerous tribes of Indians inhabited the vast wilderness lying beyond these settlements; and the British traders from Canada carried on with them a constant and lucrative traffic, to keep which, and to prevent the competition of the enterprising American trader, they used every effort to preserve the favor of the Indians, to detach them from the Americans, and to prejudice them against both the people and the Government. Intrigues were rife, for the date preceded the second war with Great Britain.

In 1805 the territory of Indiana was erected into the second grade of government. By this change the people advanced one step towards the right of suffrage and self-government. They elected the members of the popular branch of the Legislature, and the latter nominated ten persons, from which number Congress chose five, who constituted the Upper House. The Assembly thus organized appointed a delegate to Congress, who represented the Territory in that body, and was intrusted with the management of the business of the Territory. This change was urgently pressed by General Harrison, although it deprived him of much power and great patronage.

In the year 1806 the celebrated Indian, Ol-li-wa-chi-ca, the Prophet, called by some writers Els-kwa-taw-a, and his distinguished brother, Tecumseh, began to threaten the frontier of Indiana by a series of intrigues which produced the most unexpected results. Tecumseh had matured a plan to unite all the western tribes in a league against the United States, with the hope and expectation that the combined tribes would be strong enough to capture all the western settlements, and drive the settlers out of the great valley of the Mississippi and the lands north of the Ohio. The daring warrior visited the different tribes, and appealed earnestly to their patriotism, recalling the recollection of their wrongs, using in this effort the subtle diplomacy with which he was so consummately gifted, and the terse, strong oratory which, in its effect upon the tribes, reminds the reader of the battle-kindling eloquence of Demosthenes.

The two brothers, born at the same birth, differed widely in character, but were admirably fitted to act in concert in the confederation of the Nations now divided by jealousies and feuds. Tecumseh was daring and sagacious, a persuasive speaker, an able military chief, and a successful diplomatist. He was devoted to his people, and equally intense in his hatred of the white race, against whom he had sworn eternal vengeance. Peculiarly gifted with the firmness and tact which distinguishes all great leaders, full of enthusiasm, he appealed successfully both to the passions and convictions of the Indians.

The prophet had few of the manlier qualities of Tecumseh. He was not a warrior, as the Indian understood war, and was only an indifferent hunter. Haughty, crafty, and cruel, he was also indolent and selfish. Yet a variety of accidental circumstances gave him an ascendency over the tribes which his own ability could not have achieved.

The superior mind of Tecumseh had obtained a complete mastery over that of the prophet; and in council the latter rarely spoke, although a more fluent speaker than the great warrior. His manner is said to have been exceedingly graceful. Without the dignity and sagacity of Tecumseh, he advocated a more dangerous, because a more sinister, policy. Up to the year 1811 Tecumseh and his brother were engaged in constant intrigues to array the tribes against the United States. They were "in the opposition" at all the councils that were held, and earnestly endeavored to prevent every treaty that was made. Yet they carefully avoided an outbreak of hostilities before a combination could be effected. In 1808, while his brother was in Florida proposing an alliance with the Southern Indians, the prophet established his principal residence on the Wabash, near the mouth of the Tippecanoe. Here all the young warriors rallied around him, and the allies assumed a bolder and more threatening attitude. They sallied forth in greater or smaller parties, and under the pretense of hunting and visiting the neighboring tribes they were committing depredations upon, and threatening the settlers along the entire frontier.

Vincennes, the seat of government, was constantly exposed to attack; but the prophet, while he appealed to their traditions and played upon the superstition of his followers, was too indolent and too timid to enter vigorously into any aggressive action. His maladministration soon reduced the number of his adherents to less than three hundred; and these were so impoverished by their long idleness and their excesses, that they would have starved had not Governor Harrison given them a supply of provisions. The return of Tecumseh restored order.

In 1809 Governor Harrison purchased from the Delawares, Miamis, and Pottawattamies a large tract of country on both sides of the Wabash, and extending up that river about sixty miles above Vincennes. Tecumseh was away upon one of his long embassies when this sale was made. His brother, not thinking himself interested, made no opposition to the treaty; but on his return Tecumseh expressed great dissatisfaction, and threatened the chiefs who had made the treaty with death. Hearing of his displeasure, the governor invited him to come to Vincennes, and assured him "that any claims he might have to the lands which had been ceded were not affected by the treaty."

Having no confidence in the friendliness of Tecumseh, the governor insisted that he should not bring with him more than thirty warriors; but he arrived with four hundred armed followers.

The people of Vincennes were greatly alarmed, nor was the governor free from apprehension of intended treachery. The entire Territory consisted of three settlements, too far apart to rely upon each other for defensive support if the need should be sudden and imperative. In truth, if one were attacked, all were in jeopardy. The scattered population, from Kaskaskia to Kahokia, on the Mississippi; Clark's Grant, at the Falls of the Ohio; and the old French town of Vincennes, would not count quite five thousand inhabitants, all told. It is easy to reckon the number of fighting men that could be spared upon so exposed a frontier from either settlement, when all were assailable, and none had a sufficiently strong force to resist the combined tribes of the New Confederation, thickly scattered within and upon the borders of the Territory. Add to the weakness of the defensive force the threatening attitude of the Indians, who were jealous of every movement of the Americans; the wanton provocation given to the tribes by hunters and traders, who, presuming upon an enforced peace, insulted and cheated them; and last, but by no means least, the intrigues of British agents, who did not scruple to go all lengths, when occasion offered, or the possible advantage was sufficiently tempting; and it will be easy to reckon the difficulties of the position.

It is true that Governor Harrison had been invested with unlimited powers; but with "unlimited powers" very limited means had been provided for enforcing authority. The only certainty upon which the governor could count was *his unlimited responsibility in event of failure*. Such was the setting of the drama at Vincennes when the situation opened.

A large portico in front of the governor's house had been prepared for the reception. There were seats provided for the Indian leaders, as well as for the citizens who were expected to attend. Tecumseh came from his camp outside of the town, with about forty of his warriors; he stood in the grounds, refusing to enter, saying he "wished the council to be held under the shade of some trees in front of the house." As host, the governor consented to the wish of his guest.

At this council, held the 12th of August, 1810, Tecumseh, in the course of his speech, said: "Once there was no white man in all this country; then it belonged to red men, children of the same parents, placed on it by the Great Spirit, to keep it, to travel over it, to eat its fruits, and fill it with the same race; but these red men and their children have been driven from the great salt water, forced over the mountains into the prairies, away from the RIVER, which was a natural boundary; and now, if they do not resist, they will be pushed into the lakes. But they have determined to go no further. Each tribe can sell their lands, but all must join in the sale, for it requires all to make a bargain."

Governor Harrison replied: "The government had found the different tribes mentioned in the sale occupying the lands," adding that he "believed that they owned it; and it was useless to assert that the Indians were one nation, for if such had been the case, the Great Spirit would not have put six different tongues in their heads, but would have taught them all to speak one language; that the Miamis had found it for their interest to sell a part of their lands, and receive for them a further annuity."

The interpreter had scarcely finished, when Tecumseh fiercely exclaimed, "It is false!" and giving a signal to his warriors, they sprang upon their feet from the grass upon which they were sitting, seizing their war-clubs and tomahawks. The governor rose, placed his hand upon his sword, at the same time directing those of his friends and suite who were about him to stand upon their guard. Tecumseh addressed the Indians in an impassioned, earnest tone, which at times changed to what every listener felt to be fierce and violent invective.

Major Floyd, who stood near the governor, drew his dirk; Winneneak, a friendly chief, cocked his pistol; and Mr. Winans, a Methodist preacher, ran to the governor's house, seized a gun, and placed himself in the door to defend the family. For a few moments all expected a bloody ending to this first scene. But the governor kept cool, and told Tecumseh he must leave the settlement immediately.

The next morning Tecumseh, having reflected on his impolitic beginning, and, finding that he had to deal with a man as bold and vigilant as himself, apologized for the affront he had offered, and begged that the council might be renewed.

To this the governor consented, determining to leave no exertion untried to carry into effect the pacific views of the government. To prevent a repetition of the scene, he ordered two companies of militia to be placed on duty within the village. Tecumseh presented himself with the same undaunted bearing which always marked him as a chieftain; but he was now dignified and calm. The governor inquired whether he would forcibly oppose the survey of the purchase. He replied that he was determined to adhere to the OLD BOUNDARY, Then there arose a Wyandot, a Kickapoo, a Pottawattamie, an Ottawa, and a Winnebago chief, each declaring his determination to abide by Tecumseh's decision. The governor replied that "the words of Tecumseh should be reported to the President, who would take measures to enforce the treaty;" and the council ended.

The governor, still anxious to conciliate the haughty chief, went the next day to Tecumseh's camp; but beyond the cool courtesy an Indian keeps for a parley which is intended to lead to a rupture, nothing was gained by the visit.

In 1811, the near approach of a war between the United States and Great Britain excited Tecumseh's hopes, and made him more daringly determined to try conclusions with the Americans. He began to assemble a new body of warriors at the Prophet's town; he then went south to draw their new allies northward; marauding parties roved more frequently than ever towards the settlements; and a number of people were murdered on the frontiers of Indiana and Illinois. These circumstances warned the governor to place the Territory in the best attitude for defense which its limited resources would admit. Very soon he was directed by the President to move with an armed force towards the Prophet's town.

When the news reached Kentucky that Governor Harrison was authorized to march against the Indians, the public mind was excited to enthusiasm. The name of Harrison begot confidence and provoked expectation. Volunteers all along the border at once announced their readiness to follow his standard. The Fourth Regiment of United States Infantry, commanded by Colonel Boyd, was placed under his orders. The army then consisted of about nine hundred men. On the 28th of October, 1811, the troops began their march from Fort Harrison, on the Wabash, about sixty miles above Vincennes.

The advance to Tippecanoe was conducted with great prudence. The country through which the army passed was chiefly beautiful, open prairie, intersected by thick woods, overflowing creeks, and deep ravines.

To deceive the enemy, the governor caused a road to be "blazed" and partly opened, on the south side; he advanced upon it for a short distance, and then suddenly changed his route and threw his whole force across the river, to the right bank. The Indians were completely deceived by this maneuver, and their plans defeated.

On the 4th of November the army reached Pine Creek, and prepared to make the difficult crossing, which was successfully accomplished. The account of the engagement has been well described by McAffee, a gallant Kentuckian, and the following is his description, making some slight corrections from other authorities:

"On the evening of November 5th the army encamped at the distance of nine or ten miles from the Prophet's town. The traces of reconnoitering parties were very often seen; but no Indians were discovered until the troops arrived within five or six miles of the town, on the 6th of November. The interpreters were then placed with the advance guard, to endeavor to open a communication with them. The Indians only continued to insult our people by their gestures. . . .

"Being now arrived within a mile and a half of the town, and the situation being favorable for an encampment, the governor determined to remain there and fortify his camp, until he could hear from the friendly chiefs whom he had dispatched from Fort Harrison on the day he had left it, for the purpose of making another attempt to prevent hostilities. Whilst he was engaged in tracing out the lines of encampment, Major Daviess and several other field-officers urged the propriety of immediately marching on the town. But the governor wished to hear something definite from the friendly Indians whom he had dispatched from Fort Harrison. He was determined not to advance with the troops until the precise situation of the town was known; for, although it was his duty to fight when he came in contact with the enemy, it was also his duty to take care that they should not engage in an action when their valor would be useless. Major Daviess replied that, from the position of the dragoons, the openings made by the low grounds of the Wabash could be seen; that he had advanced to the bank, and had a fair view of the cultivated fields and houses of the town. Upon this information the governor said he would advance, provided he could get any proper person to go to the town with a flag.

"Captain T. Dubois, of Vincennes, having offered his services, he was dispatched with an interpreter to the Prophet, desiring to know whether he would now accept the terms that had been so often proffered. The army was moved slowly after in order of battle.

"In a few moments a messenger came from Captain Dubois informing the governor that the Indians were near him in considerable numbers, but that they would return no answer to the interpreter, although they were sufficiently near to hear what was said to them; and that, upon his advancing, they constantly endeavored to cut him off from the army.

"Governor Harrison could no longer hesitate to treat the Indians as enemies. He therefore recalled Captain Dubois, and moved forward with a determination to attack them. He had not proceeded far, however, before he was met by three Indians, one of them the principal counselor of the Prophet. They were sent, they said, to know why the army was advancing upon them; that the Prophet wished, if possible, to avoid hostilities; that he had sent a pacific message by the Miami and Pottawattamie chiefs; and that these chiefs had unfortunately gone down on the south side of the Wabash.

"A suspension of hostilities was accordingly agreed upon; and a meeting was to take place the next day between Harrison and the chiefs.

"Upon marching a short distance further the army came in view of the town, which was seen at some distance up the river upon a commanding eminence. Major Davies had mistaken some scattering houses for the town itself. The ground below the town being unfavorable for an encampment, the army marched on in the direction of the town. The dragoons being in front, soon became entangled in ground covered with brush and tops of fallen trees. A halt was ordered, and Major Davies directed to change position with Spencer's rifle corps, which occupied the open fields adjacent to the river.

"The Indians, seeing this maneuver, supposed they intended to attack the town, and immediately prepared for defense. The governor rode forward and assured them that nothing was further from his thoughts, that the ground below the town on the river was not fitted for an encampment, and that it was his intention to search for a better one above. He asked if there was any other water convenient besides the river, and was told that there was a creek two miles back to the north of the village.

"A halt was ordered, and officers sent to examine the creek returned and reported that they had found every thing that could be desirable in an encampment. The army now marched to the place selected, and encamped late in the evening, on a dry piece of ground. The order given to the army, in the event of a night attack, was for each corps to maintain its ground at all hazards till relieved. The dragoons were directed in such case to dismount, with their swords in hand, their pistols in their belts, and wait for orders.

INDIAN CONFLICTS.

"On the night of the 6th of November, the troops went to rest, as usual, with their clothes and accouterments on, and their arms by their sides. The officers were ordered to sleep in the same manner, and it was the governor's invariable practice to be ready to mount a horse at a moment's warning. On the following morning he arose at a quarter to four, and sat by the fire conversing with the gentlemen of his family. At this moment the attack commenced.

"The treacherous Indians had crept up so near the sentries as to hear them challenge when relieved. They intended to rush upon the sentries and kill them before they could fire; but one discovered an Indian creeping in the grass, and fired. This was immediately followed by an Indian yell, and a desperate charge upon the left flank. Captain Barton's company of regulars and Captain Guiger's company of mounted riflemen received the first onset. But the troops, who had lain on their arms, were immediately prepared to receive, and gallantly to resist, the furious savage assailants. The manner of the attack was calculated to terrify the men, but they maintained their ground with desperate valor.

"Upon the first alarm the governor mounted his horse, and proceeded towards the point of attack, and finding the line much weakened there, he ordered two companies from the center of the rear line to march up and form across the angle in the rear of Barton's and Guiger's companies. In passing through the camp towards the left of the front line, he was informed by Major Davies that the Indians, concealed behind the trees near the line, were annoying the troops very severely in that quarter, and requested permission to dislodge them. In attempting this charge, Davies fell, mortally wounded, as also did Colonel Isaac White, of Indiana.

"In the meantime the attack on the companies on the right became very severe. Captain Spencer was killed, with his lieutenants, and Captain Warwick mortally wounded. The governor, in passing towards that flank, led Captain Robb's company to the aid of Captain Spencer, where they fought bravely, having seventeen men killed during the battle. While the governor was leading this company into action, Colonel Owen, his aid, was killed at his side. He was shot by one of the Indians who broke through the lines, and who doubtless mistook him for the governor, as he was mounted on a gray horse, the color of Harrison's, but in the sudden surprise, Harrison had mounted the first horse he could get, which was not his old gray.

"Soon after Davies was wounded, Captain Snelling, by order of the governor, charged upon the same Indians, and dislodged them with considerable loss. The battle was now maintained on all sides with determined courage. When the day dawned, the troops drove the enemy into a swamp, through which the cavalry could not pursue them. At the same time Cook's and Lieutenant Larrabee's companies, with the aid of the riflemen and militia, charged the Indians, and put them to flight in that quarter, which terminated the battle.

"During the time of the contest, the Prophet kept himself secure on an adjacent eminence, singing a war-song.

"Tecumseh was not present at this engagement, not having yet returned from his trip to Georgia and Florida."

The victory of Tippecanoe was the most decisive battle that had yet been fought between the Indians and the Western troops. The Indians were completely routed, and their losses were unusually great, both in killed and wounded. The importance of this success is outlined in a message to Congress from President Madison:

"While it is deeply to be lamented that so many valuable lives have been lost in the action which took place on the 9th ult., Congress will see with satisfaction the dauntless spirit and fortitude victoriously displayed by every description of troops engaged, as well as the collected firmness which distinguished their commander on an occasion requiring the utmost exertion of valor and discipline."

The Legislatures of Indiana and Kentucky also passed like resolutions, declaring that "Governor William Henry Harrison behaved like a hero, a patriot, and a general, and for his cool, deliberate, skillful, and gallant conduct in the late battle of Tippecanoe, deserves the warmest thanks of the nation." One of the early writers of Ohio says:

"The news from the army was received with joy and gratitude. Every town, village, and hamlet in the Valley of the Ohio joined in the universal demonstration of thanks to the troops and their commander. The country was wild with delight; and women met the returning soldiers with the heart-felt welcome of mothers who believed that their children were now safe from the tomahawk and the scalping-knife. This victory restored confidence to the timid and composure to the fearful. The frontiersmen knew how different would have been the scene had the Prophet been the conqueror. Through the light of these fears it is easy to understand how, and why, Harrison was ever afterwards firmly placed in the hearts of the people of the North-west."

The apparent calm which succeeded the battle of Tippecanoe was not altogether a presage of peace, but rather the heavy silence which foretells a coming storm. The Indians were defeated, but they were not conciliated; a crisis in the already strained relations existing between Great Britain and the United States was imminent.

Tecumseh, apprised of the situation, renewed his efforts to bring about the confederation of the Nations, which had seemed almost hopeless immediately after the defeat of the Prophet at Tippecanoe. *That* disaster would have been impossible if the Great Chief had not been absent, for his sagacity equaled his courage. But in each of these long, forced expeditions his brother, when left in command, either through the rash persistence of some young, imprudent follower, or led by his overweening vanity to believe himself a strategist superior to Tecumseh, never failed to precipitate the outbreak which Tecumseh had strenuously labored to avoid until his allies were ready and a sure occasion presented itself to retake all the lands the tribes had lost, and regain the one boundary which they had never relinquished, the OHIO RIVER.

The United States declared war against Great Britain, June 18, 1812. The people of the North-west naturally looked to Harrison as their leader. It was an obvious fact that the first blow would be struck in the West. And so public expectation was, in a measure, prepared for the losses that came through Hull's surrender; and, just as naturally, the people believed that Harrison could and would retrieve those losses, and prevent the wide-spread savage onslaught that was again threatened. They had not forgotten that he was a prudent as well as a gallant soldier. The common danger swept away all regard for forms and precedents. Governor Scott, of Kentucky, gave Harrison a commission as major-general in the Kentucky militia, and at the head of seven thousand Kentuckians he marched northward to regain what Hull had lost.

For ten days Fort Wayne had been besieged by the Indians. At Harrison's approach they retired without waiting to hazard a battle. The Kentucky militia were hardly encamped when a United States officer arrived to take command of the army. He outranked the militia general Kentucky had created, and the camp was in a ferment of discontent, refusing to fight under any leader but the one their governor had appointed, and whom they had fought with and under from the time of Wayne's victory to the temporary truce given to the Indian question at Tippecanoe. Harrison himself persuaded them into acceptance of the new order of things, and they consented to serve under Winchester until their remonstrance could be sent in, and the War Department heard from. They had not long to wait before President Madison relieved General Winchester of the command, and appointed Harrison as general-in-chief of the North-western army.

The wisdom of this new appointment was soon seen in the improved disposition of the troops; and it was still more conclusively proven by Winchester's ill-success in a separate command, and the terrible massacre of his men at the river Raisin. After sustaining a furious assault against overpowering numbers of the British and their Indian allies, Winchester's line was broken and scattered, and the Indians began a horrible butchery. One hundred and twenty prisoners were slaughtered in one spot. Graves's division surrendered to Proctor on a pledge of security, and the larger number were killed within sight of Proctor's head-quarters.

General Harrison, hearing at the Rapids of the attack upon Winchester's camp, hastened to his relief with all the available force that was within his reach. They were met by the fugitives that had escaped, who told them of Winchester's total defeat. Leaving a strong scouting party to bring in the fugitives, the troops returned to the Rapids.

The force at the Rapids now amounted to less than nine hundred effective men. The commander fell back to Portage River, eighteen miles distant, and threw up intrenchments; but being re-enforced by General Leftwich with the Virginia brigade and a battery, they again retook their former position at the Rapids, which was strongly fortified and called Camp Meigs.

Every family in Kentucky suffered some loss at the massacre of the Raisin. The fighting temper of her people was never more severely tried and never showed firmer endurance. When the news reached Frankfort the Legislature was in session, and the governor signed a bill that day "to raise three thousand volunteers to replace those lost in the inhuman butchery at the river Raisin." The mothers, wives, and sisters of the dead made the clothing and tents for the new recruits, that were so needed at Fort Meigs, which Harrison was holding against a force of six hundred British regulars, eight hundred Canadian militia, and eighteen hundred Indians led by Tecumseh in person.

It would be impossible, in such brief space, to tell the story of that heroic defense as it should be told. The British and Indians appeared before the fort on the 26th of April, and on the 1st of May their batteries were in place, and the bombardment began. It lasted for eight days, and during that time the American loss was small. The third day the besiegers appeared to work slowly, and the garrison mounted the earth-works and cheered them on. On the night of the 3d the British erected a gun and mortar battery on the left bank of the river, within two hundred and fifty yards of the American lines. The Indians climbed into trees near the fort and poured a steady fire into the garrison. In this situation Harrison received from Proctor a summons to surrender, which was answered promptly by this refusal:

"I believe I have a very correct idea of General Proctor's force; it is not such as to create the least apprehension for the result of the contest, whatever shape he may be hereafter pleased to give it. Assure the general that he will never have this post *surrendered* to him upon any terms. Should it fall into his hands, it will be in a manner calculated to do him more honor, and to give him larger claims upon the gratitude of his government, than any capitulation could possibly do."

At twelve o'clock the following night General Green Clay, with twelve hundred Kentuckians, reached the Maumee Rapids, and sent Captain Leslie Combs to communicate with General Harrison. When within a mile of the fort, Captain Combs was attacked by the Indians and obliged to retreat, after the loss of nearly all his men. Young William Oliver managed to crawl through the Indians, and reached the fort before midnight, with the news of General Clay's speedy arrival.

Harrison now determined on a general attack, and sent orders to Clay to "land eight hundred men on the right bank, take the battery, and spike the guns." The remainder were ordered to "land on the left bank, and fight their way to the fort." General Clay descended the river as ordered, each officer taking position according to his rank. Colonel Dudley led the van, and landed on the right bank without difficulty. The violence of the current on the rapids prevented the orders being strictly obeyed. Clay landed on the left bank, with only fifty men, and fought his way into the fort. Two *sorties* were made from the garrison, one on the left, in aid of Colonel Boswell, by which the Canadian militia and Indians were defeated, and he enabled to reach the fort in safety; and one on the right, against the British batteries, which was also successful.

Dudley's detachment " drove the British from their batteries and spiked the cannon ;" but although repeatedly recalled by their officers, the men pursued the enemy and were drawn into an ambuscade, where they were surrounded by British regulars and Indians, and their retreat prevented. They were " huddled together in an unresisting crowd, and obliged to surrender." Fortunately for them, Tecumseh commanded. The Indians, with five hundred prisoners at their mercy, began a massacre. Tecumseh ordered it stopped, and killed a chief who refused to obey the order. Of the eight hundred, only one hundred and fifty escaped.

On the 9th of May Proctor raised the siege, and hurried to Malden. After that, Tecumseh was repeatedly seen near the fort, grave, stern, and splendidly mounted. "He seemed to be taking a very calm and deliberate survey of our works." One of the captives saved by Tecumseh thus described the chief:

"This celebrated man was a noble, dignified personage. He wore an elegant broadsword, and was dressed as an Indian warrior. His face was finely proportioned, his nose inclined to the aquiline, and his eyes had none of the savage and ferocious triumph common to the other Indians. He regarded us with unmoved composure, and I thought a beam of mercy shone in his countenance. I never saw him again."

The history, as continued by the captive, shows so clearly the nearness of the tragic and the comic, that we insert it.

"On our march to the garrison the Indians began to strip us. One took my hat, another my hunting-shirt, a third my waistcoat, until I was left with only my undershirt and breeches. Having read, when a boy, Smith's narrative of his life among the Indians, my idea of their character was that they treated those best who appeared most fearless. Under that impression, as we marched into the garrison, I looked at the Indians we met with all the sternness of countenance I could command. I soon caught the eye of a stout warrior, painted a lively red. He gazed as fiercely at me as I did at him, until I came within reach, when, with a contemptuous grunt, he gave me a cut over the nose and cheek-bone with his wiping-stick, which made me abandon the notion acquired from Smith; and I afterwards made as little display of hauteur and defiance as possible."

General Harrison repaired the fort, and then, leaving General Clay in command, left for Lower Sandusky, to organize the new levies. He had not been long absent before the garrison understood the meaning of Tecumseh's "calm and deliberate" inspection. July the 20th the enemy were discovered ascending the river. A party of ten men, out on a scout, were surprised by Indians in the woods, and only three escaped.

The force which began the second siege of Fort Meigs comprised five thousand men, under Proctor and Tecumseh (who now wore the uniform of a British general); the number of Indians was greater than any ever before assembled under these commanders. Toward evening the British regulars were posted in the ravine below the fort, and the cavalry in the woods above, while the Indians were on the Sandusky road. Just before dark a roar of musketry indicated a severe battle. It was so skillfully shammed that the garrison flew to arms, and even the officers of all grades insisted on marching to the assistance of the re-enforcement they believed to be on the road. It was not without great difficulty that General Clay convinced them it was only a stratagem of the enemy. Fortunately a very heavy storm and pouring rain put an end to the battle.

The next day the British regulars were gone, and the Indians soon disappeared. A few days after, they attempted to carry Fort Stephenson by assault, and were most gallantly repulsed by Major George Croghan, of whom General Harrison says in his official report: "It will not be among the least of General Proctor's mortifications that he has been baffled by a youth who has just passed his twenty-first year. He is, however, a hero worthy of his gallant uncle, General George Rogers Clark."

From this time on, to the day of his brilliant victory of the "Thames," General Harrison scored a succession of triumphs. The British, soon after their second failure at Fort Meigs, concentrated all their force at Malden. Many of the Indians, dispirited by numerous defeats, became discontented, and little parties were constantly leaving for the upper lakes, where "the hunting season had begun." All that remained were the tribes who were under the direct command of Tecumseh.

Thus far Harrison's campaign had been a purely defensive one; but the time had come to change this Fabian policy and assume the aggressive. He could not permit the enemy to rest in security after their return from a campaign of invasion. He too was ready to "carry the war into Africa." His purpose now was to capture Malden and conquer Upper Canada.

On the 20th of July, 1813, General Harrison was informed that the naval armament, built under Perry's superintendence, was ready for action. On the 2d of August Perry took his fleet over the bar at the mouth of the harbor, and sailed for Sandusky, to get his orders from the commanding general. Harrison directed him to proceed at once to Malden, and to bring the enemy to battle, as he (Harrison) believed the British commander was waiting to attack the fleet while it was engaged in the transportation of the troops to Canada.

On the 12th, Harrison, writing to Governor Shelby, says:

"Our fleet has undoubtedly met that of the enemy. The day before yesterday a tremendous and incessant cannonade was heard in the direction of Malden; it lasted two hours. I am all anxiety for the event."

Before the messenger was out of sight with the letter, came one from Perry:

"U. S. Brig 'Niagara,' off the Western Sisters,
September 10, 1813—4 P. M.

"Dear General,—We have met the enemy, and they are ours—two ships, two brigs, one schooner, and a sloop. Yours, with great respect and esteem,   Oliver Hazard Perry.
"General W. H. Harrison."

On the 20th of September General Harrison embarked with the regular troops, under Generals McArthur and Cass, and the remainder of the army followed to Put-in-Bay. On the 26th he sailed with Commodore Perry, in the *Ariel*, to reconnoiter Malden. On the 27th the army embarked, and proceeded towards the Canada shore. They landed in high spirits; but not an enemy was to be seen. The inhabitants of Canada had fled from their houses, and hid their property. The enemy was overtaken on the 5th of October.

"His right flank was covered by a swamp supposed to be impassable; his left, drawn up by the river Thames, was supported by artillery; while the Indians, two thousand strong, were posted on the right of the British regulars, and commanded by Tecumseh.

"General Harrison drew up one division of his infantry in a double line, reaching from the river to the swamp, opposite Proctor's troops; and the other division at right angles to the first, with its front extending along the swamp. The mounted Kentuckians, under Colonel Johnson, were placed in front of the infantry, General Harrison himself at the head of the front line. When Perry, who served as his aid-de-camp, remonstrated with him on this imprudence as a general, he replied: 'It is necessary that a general should set the example.' Just then Colonel Wood reported that the infantry of the enemy was formed in open column. (A space of five feet between the ranks.) Harrison instantly changed his order of attack, and directed a charge of the mounted men, with orders to form in two charging columns, and on receiving the enemy's fire, to charge through their ranks, and act as circumstances seemed to require."

The cavalry were thrown into a momentary confusion when the British infantry fired; the horses were badly frightened, which gave the British time to reload; but when the column was fairly in motion, they rode down the enemy. Forming again in their rear, the cavalry charged through and through the flying troops, and the victory was virtually won. After the rout of the regulars, there was skirmishing on the left wing, when Harrison ordered Colonel Richard M. Johnson to cross the swamp and attack the Indians. Here for a short time the conflict was obstinate and the defense determined; but Tecumseh's death ended the battle, and, in fact, ended the war on the Northwest frontier.

It was the death of the Indian Confederation, and the crowning victory of the man the North-west delighted to honor; the man "who never forgot a friend;" the "general who never lost a battle"—*that* was the proud boast of the Whigs in 1840. At this date his best claim to remembrance and honor is, "that he was just to the Indian in peace, and a fair, honorable, and merciful enemy in a war that was stained by cruelty and hate."

The region in which Tecumseh fought his last battles was also the scene of Pontiac's struggle. Both fought for admitted rights, which had been recognized in treaty after treaty; fought for their lost lands and the RIVER BOUNDARY; fought the same foes—the grim fighters of Kentucky, and those steadfast Saxons, descendants of the old Colonial Virginians, who had stood by the KING or Cromwell in the "brave days of old." Of all the martial figures that have gone down before this "fighting contingent," none showed greater prowess in the field, none were wiser in council, none more daringly rash in action, none more devoted to the union of a nation and the glory of a race than the great chieftain who fell beside the Thames—fighting for his people, and their right to the north shore of THE BRIGHT SHINING RIVER.*

*Appendix A, No. V.

C. M. C.

PART SECOND.

Afloat on the Deep, Shining River.

FROM PITTSBURG TO CAIRO

ON

The Ohio.

Afloat on the Deep Shining River.

NOTWITHSTANDING the rapidly increasing threads of the immense railway systems which are constantly being woven into a chain-work of steel and iron, up and down and across the river—from Pittsburgh to Cairo—its waters still bear bravely a noble fleet of STEAMERS.

Each city on the Ohio has its system of regular "packets." And although the palmy days are gone, when one steamboat brought the rich gifts of fortune to owners and officers, there are very certain and comforting gains yet to be gathered by the happy holders of "stock in a Packet Company."

In the early days of steamboating ventures, a village on the Ohio, or sometimes a neighborhood landing-place, "owned a boat," which, from the "pilot-house" to the "lower deck," was officered and occasionally manned by the owners or their kinsmen. Sturdy fellows and true were these "boatmen"—unlettered, yet frequently the lucky owners of that more profitable learning which use doth breed. They were, in the main, untaught of schools or books, and had but slight respect for a man who got all he knew from such uncertain sources. They were not gentlemen, in the circumscribed sense; yet they were *not at all unmannered men*, for they united to courage gentleness. Granted that they were sometimes compelled by stress of circumstance, to knock down a refractory "deck-hand," or quiet with harsh voice a roystering "roustabout;" nevertheless, when that urgent duty was done, they were courteous, attentive, and gallant to every woman, young or old, who set foot upon the " gangway." Besides, they were the tenderest and most indulgent comrades of the small travelers, who, with that peculiar occult understanding of the child-mind, soon discovered that the vantage ground of baby-independence was found when a small autocrat set foot on the "hurricane deck," or outran the nurse in a race forward.

But "other times, other manners." The old-fashioned steamboatmen—may Heaven keep them from avarice or purse-pride!—have left the RIVER, to put government bonds in Safe-Deposits. Yet, in view of the changed conditions, we feel ready to wager our last shilling that those hapless and miserable millionares are walking sadly through the "marble halls" of an effete (or mushroom) aristocracy, sighing for the lost freedom of the "upper deck," and longing for the satisfying banquets of "Texas."

The old-time pilots trained in the schools which required daring as well as doing, are still in their old places; for their gains were less, and their skill was so wonderful, and their courage so constant that they could not be spared from the "pilot-house."

The course of the Ohio is a very crooked one. From Pittsburgh it takes a north-west direction for about twenty-five miles, then turns in gradual inflections west—south—west, following this general direction for nearly five hundred miles, when it bends more decidedly to the south-west for one hundred and sixty miles, then almost due west in easy serpentine curves to where it joins the Mississippi in a south-east course, latitude 36° 46′, eleven hundred miles below its source. The dangers and difficulties of this tortuous course are increased when the uncertain currents of its lower tributaries increase the volume of its waters; and the floods fill up or wash out the river-bed into new channels. In addition to these opposing forces in its lower lengths, the river has numerous islands—fifty within a distance of three hundred and ninety miles. Its banks are low where the hills recede from the water, leaving wide stretches of bottom-lands which are subject to heavy inundations when a late spring and frequent rains bring the melting snows in swelling torrents down from the mountains.

Yet let the wind " blow high or blow low," let the floods come, let the tricky river play at hide-and-seek with its channel, the skill of the pilot is rarely at fault. Master of the wheel, he calmly faces the situation and holds his own.

The Ohio has two regular seasons of

high water, the spring floods varying in date from the last of February to May, and even so late as June; and the autumn "rises," from October to early December.

From DUQUESNE HEIGHTS, at Pittsburgh, one has a commanding view of the junction of the Allegheny and the Monongahela. There are charming border stretches up the valleys of the formative affluents, and a wonderful breadth of effect where the Ohio sweeps its collected streams around Davis Island. If one sees this striking river-view in the clear and pure outline, in the precise distinctness of dawn, or when the setting sun lights the reflective waters with resplendent color, it is fixed in the mind for all after days. To an imaginative person the scene is most attractive at night; for it seems "a faëry vision," when the natural-gas torches are aflame with the New World's exhibit of the "Holy Fires of Baku."

The story of the Ohio has a certain mystic and poetic background which gives it a striking and weird significance in the chronicles of the last two centuries, altogether different from the tame and commonplace annals of other gentle-flowing streams.

The RIVER has not only been the scene of dramatic incidents, but it has also been the cause of leading events. In the various conflicts for its possession, and in the successive tragedies enacted upon its banks, it was not merely

"Part of the fateful setting of the play,"

but an actual Character in a series of occurrences to which it lends the investiture of dramatic unity. In the legends of the Western Indians, who fought for it with such persistence and relinquished it with such bitterness, it ranks as a Personage, and in their traditional stories it bears a strangely grotesque likeness to the fabled river gods of classic Greece.

The streams running into the Ohio have rich bottom-lands, which are easy of culture, but nothing could excel the fertility of the River's banks. Michaux, the eminent French naturalist, who went down the Ohio in 1803, says:

"The soil is a true vegetable earth produced by the thick bed of leaves annually collected on the ground for centuries, and converted into mould by the prevalent humidity. Additions have been made to these successive beds of vegetable earth from the trunks of enormous trees destroyed by age. . . . I have seen nothing to be compared to the vegetative power of these forests."

He gives the measure of a plane-tree (*Platanus occidentalis*), the circumference of which, at five feet above the ground, was forty feet and four inches—about thirteen feet in diameter. He adds: "General Washington measured this same tree fifty years ago."

The forests that edge the southern affluents of the Ohio, and cover the overlooking heights, are grouped into colonies of soft and hard wood—of willow, poplar, sycamore, gum, maple, walnut, cherry, ash, hickory, and oak; while above all, and over all, tower unnumbered acres of pine and cedar.

There are nowhere any wide, billowy prairies, rolling backward from the Ohio, yet the narrowness of the landscape only adds a more striking and definite effect to the presentations offered in the long successive miles of alternating cities, villages, farms, and forests upon its banks. Its marginal stretches of uncultivated woodlands show a richness of coloring, a magnificence of growth, a luxuriance of hanging vine and flowering shrub, that belong of right only to a virgin forest, and yet this unspoiled wilderness of shade that lends its most perfect charm to the river is, in the main, a voluntary growth of the last twenty years.

Then, again, the river is unlike all others in its constant reproduction of certain characteristics. From Pittsburgh to Cairo its individuality is never lost. The graceful curves continue their sentinel line of unending, yet ever-changing, linked and rounded hills, which stretch from the out-pushing spurs of the Allegheny Mountains, to where the Mississippi sweeps its solemn floods by the little city which is yet to be the Queen, as it is now the Gateway of Rivers—never losing the glittering continuity of its water-reflected chain.

Situated at the head of this remarkable system of inland navigation, PITTSBURGH reaches by river transportation eighteen States and two Territories, while it also stands as the center of railway systems that radiate to all points of the compass. Along the Allegheny, Monongahela, and Ohio Rivers, for some distance from Pittsburgh, shipment direct from the factories is daily practiced; and the increasing demand for cheap transportation, encouraging the rivalry between the natural water-ways and the railway-systems, will finally cause all the navigable affluents of the River to be made as available for transport as engineering skill can render them.

The OHIO is a continuation of the Monongahela, and not of the Allegheny, which arrives at the conflux in an oblique direction, and is a swifter, as well as a clearer, stream than the larger southern affluent. From the very force and swiftness of its descent from the uplands, the Allegheny was always comparatively free from obstructions to navigation, while the sluggish Monongahela has been opened by a system of locks, ending at Davis Island Dam, which effectually protects it from the aggressive incursions of the Allegheny. Nine bridges link Allegheny City and Pittsburgh, and five span the Monongahela.

Fort Pitt, built by the troops, was finished about the 1st of January, 1759. The French, from Venango, were preparing to undertake its reconquest. However, hearing that Sir William Johnson was marching against Fort Niagara, they were diverted from their undertaking. At this opportune moment General John Stanwix presents himself in the list of memorable historical names. He was chief engineer in constructing the defensive works, of which he says in a letter dated September 24th: "It will to latest posterity secure the British empire on the Ohio." Washington writes, in 1770, criticising its construction which was afterwards partially remedied.

In 1760 the works were reported completed from the Allegheny to the Monongahela, and they cost the British Government £60,000 sterling. Fifteen years later it was abandoned by order of the British Government, and now nothing of Fort Pitt remains, and the only memorial of the British possession of the Mississippi Valley is a single "redoubt," built in 1764 by Colonel Bouquet, outside the fort, now used as a dwelling. It was probably soon after the Battle of Bushy Run that Colonel Bouquet built the "redoubt" (1764), and in the same year Colonel John Campbell laid out that part of Pittsburgh bounded by Water, Second, Ferry, and Market Streets. From this time forward the fort was the scene of Indian treaties rather than battles, and the point of departure for various expeditions against the hostile tribes. The growth of the incipient town was slow, and the early allusions to it are far from being complimentary or prophetic of the greatness which it has attained; indeed, its inhabitants were spoken of in 1766 as living in "some kind of a town without the fort;" and in 1770 the log houses are said by Colonel Washington to be about twenty in number, and inhabited by Indian traders. The ramparts of the fort were still standing in 1796; but in the meantime another smaller fortification had been erected by Major Isaac Craig, called Fort La Fayette. The survey of the "Manor of Pittsburgh" was authorized on January 5, 1769, and the lands embraced within it were five thousand nine hundred and sixty-six acres. In the fall of 1783, the two proprietors, J. Penn and J. Penn, Jr., determined to sell tracts to the "Manor," and in January, 1784, the first sale of lands within the boundaries of Pittsburgh was made to Isaac Craig and Stephen Bayard. Lots were quickly sold, and the era of development began. In *Niles' Register*, the town is reported to have, in 1786, thirty-six log houses, and one stone and one frame house, making a population of three hundred and eighty, leaving, of course, the garrison of the fort out of consideration. In 1788, Dr. Hildreth says: "Pittsburgh then contained four hundred or five hundred inhabitants, several retail stores, and a single garrison of troops in old Fort Pitt. To our travelers (the pioneers of the multitude that afterwards passed through the gateway of the 'Beautiful River'), who had lately seen nothing but trees and rocks, with here and there a solitary hut, it seemed to be quite a large town. The houses were chiefly built of logs, but now and then one had assumed the appearance of neatness and comfort."

In 1796 the borough contained 1,395 people; of these, a few years later, Mr. Neville B. Craig could only enumerate one hundred and two houses standing in the Pittsburgh of 1796. The city, incorporated March 18, 1816, attained a population in 1820 of 7,248, and from that time onward the decades of its

LOOKING UP ELK CREEK.
(CHARLESTON, W. VA.)

growth have been as follows: In 1830, 12,568; in 1840, 21,115; in 1850, 46,616; in 1860, 49,217; in 1870, 89,076; in 1880, 156,381; in 1890, 238,473; and during this time the city of Allegheny grew apace with Pittsburgh, separated from it by the Allegheny River. So in the brief interval—measuring time by history—of one hundred and thirty-two years, peace has succeeded war. Now the battle of industry is being incessantly fought, and with greater success than the former ones, though filling the air with smoke and steam instead of powder.

The Pittsburgh of to-day shows the immense advantages of its position in the leading iron and steel producing county of the United States, that of Allegheny. Well named the "Gateway of the West," its situation in respect of water interests, at the fork formed by the Allegheny and the Monongahela Rivers where they meet and flow into the Ohio, gives it a trade on that river rivaling in extent and importance the entire foreign commerce of the United States. So as to make the Allegheny River an extension of the Ohio for thirty miles, two or three dams have been constructed, and the vast aggregation of manufactories and work-shops of Pittsburgh and adjacent country, really constitute an arsenal for the creation of war material of all sorts second to no other point in the country. In every war fought by the United States, Pittsburgh has been a vital point of supply. Over four thousand cannons have been manufactured here for the use of the Government, many of them of the heaviest caliber known at the time.

From the date of the construction of the "New Orleans," in 1811, until the present time, steamboat-building has been a leading feature of its industries, and one steamer per week was turned out from the shops and boat-yards for a quarter of a century, beginning with the year 1842. Also in most of that period, half the steam-fleet navigating Western waters was Pittsburgh built, and the progress made in skill and science of construction was largely drawn upon when the demands of the war required craft of novel designs and purposes. Incidental thereto was the devising of steamers capable of towing coal-boats and barges. Experience tempted the river men, when once the efficacy of lashing boats together rigidly, and to the stern-wheeler's front, was established, to go on increasing the power of engines and steering apparatus, so that now Pittsburgh has steamers that can take twenty thousand tons of coal to market, a cargo greater than the "Great Eastern" ever handled, and, what is of far more importance, the expense of transportation is lower than by any other system of carrying in the world.

The amount of coal shipped from here alone is enough to place Pittsburgh among the leading ports of the world. Her tonnage embraces at least four thousand one hundred barges, boats, and "flats," and their money value, added to the steam-fleet, makes a total investment of $10,000,000.

The commencement of the maunfacture of *iron* in Western Pennsylvania dates back to the year 1790, and the pig-iron industry of Pittsburgh has been highly successful in the last quarter of a century. The center of production for the whole continent now lies very probably within the limits of Pittsburgh. The iron and steel trades have grown rapidly since the introduction of natural gas.

The following extracts from the *Ohio Valley Manufacturer* will show the importance of the Bessemer invention: "The casting of the great Bessemer steel gun for the United States government at the works of the Pittsburgh Steel Casting

Company was a success. Sixteen thousand five hundred pounds of melted iron were used; sixty men were employed in the operation one hour and thirty-seven minutes. The great importance of this experiment consists in the fact that the gun cast under this new method will cost $3,300, while the built-up gun, under the old method, would cost $22,000.

These Bessemer steel plants will steadily increase in value to the full net profit to the country of $100,000,000 a year, not a dollar of which goes out of the country and not a dollar of which is lost. This $100,000,000 will be distributed along the lines of new railways, along the sources of coke and coal, with the transportation by rail and steamboat, and in the mines, and with their owners and laborers, and ten years hence the country will be worth $1,000,000,000 more for it."

No large interest in which local capital is concerned has grown more rapidly within recent years than the manufacture of *Connellsville coke*. At the very gates of Pittsburgh and tributary to her commerce, are located the interesting and unique coke-making regions of Western Pennsylvania. The one product of this limited area is coke, a commercial fuel which is sought for by iron founders and smelters from Lake Champlain and New York on the east, to Salt Lake and Omaha on the west, and from Canada to the Gulf of Mexico. Coke is the product of slow combustion applied to the soft bituminous coal of the region.

This coal is a well-defined portion of the "Pittsburgh coal-basin," the vein varying in thickness from 8 to 11 feet, and worked at all depths below the surface of the ground down to 300 feet. The entire deposit of coal lies to the south-east of Pittsburgh, and varies in width from two to twelve miles, with a length of about forty miles. Mining engineers have explored every coal-bearing region of the country for a coal identical with Pittsburgh's Connellsville coking coal. Though its discovery would be worth untold millions, their efforts have been vain.

Glass making is, perhaps, Pittsburgh's oldest industry, and has grown to be of prime importance in her general industrial account. It was established here in 1795, among the first in the country, and was, in addition, remarkable in that it was the first also in the United States in the use of coal as fuel. There are now in operation in the district a large number of glass factories of all classes, including several for the manufacture of plate-glass. Many millions of glass bottles and flasks are produced annually, including a large proportion of the flint-glass prescription bottles used by the physicians of the country. Pittsburgh also supplies most of the lamp-chimneys used in the United States.

The recent substitution of natural gas for coal in all the processes of glass-making has had a beneficial effect, which can not be estimated. Because of its purity and freedom from sulphur, the glass produced with it is better in every way, perfectly free from flaw or speck, and adding to the attractiveness of the table by the peculiar brilliancy and beauty of the pressed ware. With natural gas the finest plate-glass in the world is produced, and that of Pittsburgh is rapidly superseding all others in our American markets. Formerly it was difficult to sell plate-glass of American manufacture, and it was necessary to counterfeit the stamps of foreign manufacturers in order to procure a sale for it. The superiority of the home-made plate-glass is now acknowledged, thanks to natural gas, and the factories are unable to keep up with the demand, though running to their full capacity.

The chief industries of Pittsburgh, glass, iron, and steel.

speak for themselves. Skilled artisans can easily find employment here for almost every specialty now turned out in the Old World, and the growing and wide-spread desire for fine goods all over the great West and the reviving South, are important elements in the calculation of those who consider the fact that these regions have for years been in the habit of looking to Pittsburgh for their glass-ware. Where the window-glass for a quarter of a million of houses is made; where ninety millions of bottles and vials, twelve millions of tumblers, and forty millions of lamp-chimneys are manufactured every year, there is also the place for the production of colored and cut glasses to rival Murano, Belgium, and Bohemia.

Enough has been said to show the importance of Pittsburgh as the first in the list of cities and towns on the Ohio River in respect of wealth and progress as well as situation. The city itself, with its well-planned streets, is interesting from its never-ceasing life and bustle. Nothing could be more fascinating, even to an amateur, than a visit to its colossal steel-works, from the great "puddling" process to which the iron is exposed to when it lies finished the most beautiful steel for every possible purpose, all by the aid of natural gas; the Bessemer Steel Works, with the wonderful invention of which so much has been said and written, to the glass-works, where hours could be passed watching the dexterity only acquired by the habits of a life-time in turning the formless mass of "spun-glass" into articles of every-day use.

About five and one-half miles below Pittsburgh is Davis Island, at the foot of which is located the first movable dam on the Ohio River. This work was commenced in August, 1878, and the system decided upon was the one that has been so successful on the Seine, Yonne, Marne, Meuse, and other French rivers, that known from its inventor as the Chanoine. Its completion was celebrated in October, 1885. The total cost of the dam was less than $900,000.

The river below Pittsburgh for the next ten miles is thickly settled. Passing Glendale, Haysville, and Sewickley, through most luxurious vegetation, Economy Village, hedged in by the rounded contours of the hills, is reached. This is the third home of the Harmony Society, who emigrated to this country in 1803 from South Germany, followers of George Rapp, the founder of this communistic society. The members own twenty-five hundred acres of the surrounding country, of which every inch is cultivated. Mr. Charles Nordhoff gives an interesting description of this society in his "Communistic Societies of the United States."

Another twenty miles bring us to the enterprising town of East Liverpool, Ohio, where several thousand men are engaged in the manufacture of porcelain and stone ware. "The veins of fire-clay on both sides of the river, between East Liverpool and Wheeling, are extensive and inexhaustible, and are proving a rich source of revenue to that section, and an important factor in the manufacturing interests of this valley. The business had a beginning in Hancock County, West Virginia, fifty-five years ago; but it is only quite recently that its importance has attracted the attention of large capitalists, whose energy and business tact are rapidly pushing it to the front of American industries. Between East Liverpool and Wheeling there are a number of these works, most of them very extensive, and many new ones are in contemplation. All are crowded with orders, and ship goods to every section of the country."

Sixty-seven miles below Pittsburgh we reach Steubenville,

Ohio, the capital of Jefferson County. This is a progressive and well-laid-out town, and wears its name in honor of Baron Steuben, of Revolutionary fame, though the fort first named after him was destroyed by fire in 1790. The town, for a time, made but slow progress, but was incorporated a city in 1851. The Ohio being at all times navigable southward from Steubenville, it is in reality the head of navigation the whole year round, as during freshets Pittsburgh and other towns above are completely isolated. More tumblers are made here than in any other city on the globe, the largest works turning out upwards of 36,000 tumblers per day. This city can also boast of the largest glass-chimney works in the world, while, as a place of residence, it presents many attractions.

Leaving Steubenville the views all along the river are particularly beautiful; the distant hills make a fine background for the shining water as it curves in and out its green banks, and at a distance of about thirteen miles from Steubenville, near Tiltonville, an Indian mound is plainly visible.*

Thirty miles further down we reach the great bridge over which the Baltimore and Ohio Railroad crosses from Ohio to Virginia, and at our left lies the beautiful city of Wheeling, in West Virginia. Wheeling is situated on an alluvial area

---

*Of these mounds Ohio alone contains 11,500, and with the earth-works, called inclosures, there are 13,000. Nothing positive is known as to the race by which these mounds were built, called Mound-builders, from the nature of the traces they left behind them. Pre-historic they certainly were, whether in the sense of antedating the discovery of America or not, remains a question that seems to admit of much discussion. These mounds are divided by different archæologists into several classes, chief among which are the military and the sacred. One of the most remarkable of these earth-works is Fort Ancient, on the east bank of the Little Miami River, 33 miles north-east of Cincinnati, and, in fact, they abound in the Ohio and Mississippi Valleys; for, with no other proof than the size and number of the mounds, the fact is established that the Mound-builders were, to a certain extent, tillers of the soil, and selected sites near the rivers, where not only was communication assured, but vegetation abounded.

or isthmus on the east side of the Ohio River, about 96 miles below Pittsburgh, and lies on both sides of Wheeling Creek, which empties into the Ohio River. The geographical position of the city combines the agricultural advantages of an inland town with all the sources of prosperity arising from navigable water-courses and great national thoroughfares. It is surrounded by bold and precipitous hills, containing almost inexhaustible seams of bituminous coal, while its location on a high elevation of ground renders it secure from inundations and ravages of high water. It nestles like a gem in its setting right amid these foot-hills of the Appalachian range, the most famous and richly-endowed coal-producing mountain range in the world. Every one of these foot-hills or spurs in the neighborhood of Wheeling is rich in coal deposits. In fact, every county in West Virginia, between the Ohio River and the Maryland and Virginia lines, is underlaid with coal in quantities and in all desirable varieties. Wheeling is, in more than one sense, the metropolitan center from which the agencies which nourish and strengthen the balance of the State radiate. She has geographical advantages and facilities which render it possible for her to become one of the notably progressive centers of the country.

Through an existence of over a century, first as an isolated settlement, far beyond the frontier; then as a fort, for the possession of which was fought the last battle of the Revolution; later a trading village, whose position on the Ohio River gave her prominence and prosperity; a town on the great National Road; after that ceased to be the great thoroughfare between the East and the West, a thriving city at the western terminus of the Baltimore & Ohio Railroad; and since a growing community, with increased facilities of communication with the world at large,—in this varied existence as village, town, and city, Wheeling has steadily held her own in the contest for the survival of the fittest.

The construction of the National Road gave to her an importance she had not possessed before. Her position as the point of tranfers for the people of the whole Western country, from the palatial steamers which plied the Ohio, to the swinging stages which climbed and descended the slopes of the Alleghenies, gave her advantages among towns of the country envied by many a larger sister. The laying of the Baltimore & Ohio track to the river assured the continuance and increase of those advantages, and the city gradually changed from a trading and shipping post to a considerable manufacturing and mercantile community, and the little town on the bluff spread out into a good city, with neighboring towns above and below and across the river. Gradually she assumed the position of the metropolis of Western Virginia; and when from the throes of civil war a new State was born, she was its only city, and she has remained among the increasing list of thriving towns of the Mountain State in manufacturing and commercial interests as well as population, far in advance of all her rivals. She has seen cities grow up in her suburbs rivaling in importance the Wheeling of less than a generation ago; and when her citizens look back over the record of enterprise and progress, increasing with the years, no era stands distinct, in beginning or ending, from the years which preceded or those which followed; for her growth has been so steady and so constant as to be almost imperceptible.

Her lanterns, her calico, her furniture, are known and used far and wide. Her iron and steel is fashioned into thousands of shapes, thousands of miles away. Her queensware from her pottery has won for the city new laurels as a manufacturing center. Her leather, her calico, her iron, and glass and china ware, have an enviable name in all parts of the country.

Beyond "McCulloch's leap," and beautifully situated in a natural amphitheater of rounded hills, is the Mount de Chantal, for more than forty years celebrated as a boarding-school, and presided over by the Sisters of the Visitation. This order was founded three hundred years ago in France, by the Baroness Jane de Chantal, grandmother of Madame de Sévigné.

The scenery below Wheeling is thoroughly typical of the Ohio River; the rolling country, the rich land, bordered with the tender green of the river willows, hanging protectingly over the banks, while at Moundsville, a distance of ten and one-half miles, another Indian mound, planted here and there with trees, overlooks the village. Further down beautiful and richly cultivated islands divide the river, and one is everywhere passing little villages.

Marietta, Ohio, is the next town of any importance. It has fine views of the Ohio and Muskingum Valleys. Situated at the junction of the Muskingum with the Ohio River, and centrally in as valuable deposits of sandstone as can be found in the country, and in one of the best agricultural counties in the State, that of Washington, Marietta has many advantages, not the least of which are those that make it a shipping port.*

---

*Marietta has, as an early and useful settlement, a certain historic importance; but in two points she overestimates her claims. Pittsburgh was a fort in the middle of the century, and a thriving village when the expedition to Marietta was planned. Geographically and historically, Pittsburgh was, and is, the Gateway of the West (which Marietta claims to be in her centennial issue). Marietta was settled by the New England successors to the title of Virginia Ohio Land Company, organized by the Lees and Washingtons. The previous battles of the Virginians and the Scotch-Irish Pennsylvanians, made peace secure, and thus was inaugurated the advent of what an early writer calls the "long-vested, stiff-collared,

Twelve miles below Marietta lies the city of Parkersburg, first called "The Point," the second city in size in West Virginia, and the county-seat of Wood, pleasantly situated on the southern bank of the Ohio, at and above the mouth of the Little Kanawha River. Here, at a cost of between two and three millions of dollars, an iron bridge has been built across the Ohio River, resting upon solid piers of stone a hundred feet above the bed of the stream, giving access to the State of Ohio, and from which a fine view can be obtained of Parkersburg, the Ohio Valley, the beautiful Island of Blennerhassett, and the heights of Fort Boreman. In December, 1800, the survey of the town of Parkersburg was completed, the streets of which are made to intersect each other at right angles, running from the Ohio River in a south-easterly direction, and from the Little Kanawha north-east. This river is a stream of considerable importance, navigable for fully twenty-eight miles, and now being surveyed so as to be navigable for sixty miles, and, with its lumber, makes the principal trade of Parkersburg, which is pre-eminently a manufacturing city.

The Island of Blennerhassett, situated in a heavy bend in the Ohio River to the west, a mile below the mouth of the Little Kanawha, and in full view of the city of Parkersburg, presents a most attractive appearance. The island now contains

---

broadcloth-clothed " New Englander. The first white man whose foot ever touched the soil of the Ohio Valley was La Salle, who reached Louisville in 1667, and would have proceeded to the Mississippi, except for the desertion of his men. He was encamped on the "Knobs," at New Albany, and made his way back by land to Lake Erie with the few Indians, who were all that remained of his original large following. Thus Louisville has a certain and established priority of date over every settlement south-west of Pittsburgh, as the town was laid out in 1777 by Thomas Bullitt; but the first settlement on the island at the mouth of "Bear Grass Creek," which, from its position, was much more secure from Indian raids, was made in 1773. This little fort was the center where the fighting contingents were collected whenever Indians were to be repulsed, or a raid of reprisal was to be made into their country, and these dates certainly outrank Marietta.

about two hundred acres of the best bottom-land of the Ohio River, and one of the best farms in this country; it is in a good state of cultivation, and possesses orchards of fine fruits, and, from its natural location and advantages, is most valuable. Ravenswood, West Virginia, is passed near the "Big Bend" of the river, and Portland, Ohio; New Haven, West Virginia; and Mason City, and, opposite, Pomeroy, Ohio, with its great salt-works, sixty-three miles below Parkersburg; then the little towns of Middleport and Sheffield. Another sixteen miles, and the Big Kanawha River empties into the Ohio at Point Pleasant, West Virginia, the scene of a memorable Indian battle in 1774.

Gallipolis, laid out by French settlers in 1791; Chambersburgh and Bladensburgh, on the right bank of the Ohio; Apple Grove and Mercerville, on the left; Millersport, Haskelville, Ohio, and Proctorville, and, opposite, Guyandotte, West Virginia, at the mouth of the Guyandotte River; and these, with Bradricksville and Frampton, Ohio, bring us to Huntington, West Virginia, a new town below the mouth of the Guyandotte River. Catlettsburg, eight miles below Huntington, is at the mouth of the Big Sandy River, which forms the Kentucky State line; and in Kentucky, at a distance of three miles, is the pretty little town of Ashland. The site possesses great natural advantages, being upon a broad plateau, sufficiently undulating to afford good natural drainage, and having as its entire front the finest deep-water harbor above Cincinnati. The survey of the town provided beautiful streets and avenues, those at right angles from the river being eighty feet wide, and those parallel to it being one hundred feet in width. It was named for the home of Henry Clay.

Nearly opposite Ashland, on the Ohio side of the river, is the very progressive town of Ironton. The town was founded by the Lawrence County iron-masters of forty years ago, as a manufacturing and shipping point for their product. The iron industry of the county, starting with the building of Union Furnace in 1826, had expanded till, in 1848, some nine charcoal-furnaces were shipping from Hanging Rock—a village lying at the foot of bold, sandstone escarpments, three miles below the present site of Ironton—a grade of iron of such admitted superiority in Western markets, as to give its name, the name of the village, to the entire region. In 1848 and 1849 the iron masters wisely organized two companies, the Iron Railroad Company, to build a line tapping the furnace region, the Ohio Iron and Coal Company, to establish a town at the railroad's river terminus. The real estate company bought three hundred and twenty-four acres, lying near the center of the broad bottom, which stretched, some seven miles long, from Hanging Rock to opposite where Ashland, Kentucky, now lies, and on it in June, 1849, laid out the town of Ironton, which was incorporated January, 1851, and the same year became the seat of Lawrence, now the most populous county on the Ohio River from the Miami to the Muskingum.

The scenery of the Ohio River is here filled with striking characteristics. The hills are more rugged, and, passing the bold ledge called Hanging Rock, wilder than at any other point, while the smoke and flame from a hundred chimneys announce the center of a great manufacturing region, Burke's Point, Wheelersburg, and Scioto Village, we reach Portsmouth, Ohio, twenty-eight miles below Ironton, one of the most interesting towns on the river, on account of its age, lying at the mouth of the Scioto River. Two miles below Portsmouth it is believed that a French fort existed as early as 1740. It is probably true that four families came down the Ohio from the Redstone settlement in 1785, and settled where Portsmouth now stands, but were driven away by the Indians. That Alexandria was built, flourished, and afterwards died, is a well-known historical fact. The land on which Portsmouth now stands was partly cleared, and a plat made for a town in 1803, but a new plat was made in 1805, and with that the town really began. The original proprietor of the patent received from government, and signed by John Adams, President, was Colonel Thomas Parker. This patent bears date of February, 1798, and the following year the town was laid out. It was supposed to be an excellent location in the large, fertile valley of the Scioto, which was selected for its agricultural advantages, but the Ohio and its great floods were then an unknown quantity, and it afterwards proved that the town plat was only fifty feet above low-water mark, so that an overflow was an annual certainty. Alexandria was of some use for the short time of its existence to persons going to Maysville and Cincinnati; so some few good buildings were erected, and one or two of these two-story stone houses were in existence long after the village had been abandoned.

Henry Massie, whose brother laid out the town of Chillicothe, purchased in 1802 several sections of lands on the east side of the Scioto, and in 1803 made the plat of Portsmouth, named for Portsmouth, Virginia, the home of the Massies in Colonial days. To get his new town settled he made several liberal offers to the Alexandrians, who, up to this time, had preferred the west bank, as the east bank was but a dreary-looking forest. A sudden flood of the Ohio convinced them that Alexandria was not a safe place of residence, and most of the families immediately crossed the river.

The death of the old town decided the prosperity of the new. Log cabins and frame dwellings were scattered over the plat, a substantial hewed log house afterwards weatherboarded, and most of the business houses were built on Front Street, then called Ohio Street; and a few of these old buildings still remain.

The settlers were principally from Virginia, West Virginia, and New Jersey, and in 1810 the population was between 300 and 400. The first court-house was finished in 1816. "The first steamboat was builded through a privilege given to Aaron Fuller by the town council to construct a steamboat on the commons in front of the town, in 1829."

In this era flourished a literary institution called the Franklin Institute, which gave giant minds a chance to expand, and inspired the weaker ones. The first of the young Ciceros, in his speech before this assembly, in eulogizing the merits of Washington, said: "He fought, bled, and died for his country, and then retired to private life." (From the History of the Lower Scioto Valley, by S. W. Cole.)

Passing a number of comparatively small villages, we reach Maysville, Kentucky, fifty-two miles below Portsmouth, and one of the prosperous river towns, settled about the same time as Cincinnati. Then the river banks become more thickly settled, and the towns of Ripley, Levanna, Dover, Higginsport, Augusta, Chilo, Neville, Point Pleasant, California, Palestine, and Columbia, are passed in rapid succession, while the hills, thickly studded with suburban homes, indicate the proximity of the Queen City, the Metropolis of the Ohio Valley.

Cincinnati, to which now is universally acceded the title of "QUEEN CITY OF THE WEST," was first known as Losantiville—the village opposite the mouth—L-os-anti-ville, more really the mouth opposite the village; so named on account of the Licking River, on the Kentucky side, of which the banks were a favorite hunting resort. Traces of occupation by an unknown race were found by the early settlers, notably a tablet on this spot—probably the grave of a mound-builder; but the first positive date recorded is that of 1780, when "Colonel George Rogers Clark, with an army of about one thousand men, crossed the Ohio at the mouth of the Licking, and erected two blockhouses, on the 1st day of August, upon the ground now occupied by Cincinnati." These served as store-houses, and in 1785 a short military settlement occurred. In 1779 Captain Robert Patterson, one of the most daring and gallant of the early frontiersmen, had built a solitary block-house where now is the center of Lexington, Kentucky; and in the winter of 1788–89, with Denman and Israel Ludlow, he laid out the town of Losantiville. In September of the same year, at the instigation of the officer in command, the site of Fort Washington was changed from North Bend to Losantiville, which, after St. Clair's defeat, became the head-quarters of the North-western Territory. By the close of 1789, eleven families and twenty-four unmarried men were residents of the village; and in 1790, "Cincinnati began to live, and Losantiville was no more." In 1800 the village was composed of a few frame and log houses, with a population of seven hundred and fifty inhabitants; and in 1808 the fort was condemned and ordered to be sold.

The *Centinel of the North-western Territory* was the first newspaper published north of the Ohio River, in 1793, and

BRIDGE OVER THE RAVINE.

already in early days Cincinnati stood pre-eminent as the book market of the West, the distributing point for the entire Valley of the Mississippi. The first book-store in the city was opened in 1819.

In 1812 Fulton introduced steamboats on the Ohio, and in 1816 the first steamboat was built in Cincinnati. With the growth of steamboat-building Cincinnati at once became the center of a vast commerce, and traded with the most distant parts of the Mississippi Valley. The number of steamboats built in Cincinnati amounted to one-fifth of the whole number built in the United States, and she became the point of receipt and distribution of the immense surplus products of a great region. To this large steamboat commerce is also due the fact that Cincinnati had for many years a population of prosperous river-men, growing rich, year by year, from the enormous river-traffic, and, beginning with positions on the boats plying to and fro on the Ohio, retired middle-aged men, possessed of handsome fortunes.

From "an early visit to Cincinnati," we learn that in 1823 "there were no houses where Newport and Covington now are, and the city hardly reached above Second Street, parallel with the Ohio River. The principal buildings were on the street perpendicular to the upper river wharf, on the right of which was the hotel. There were few brick buildings, and on Second and Third Streets the houses were few and scattering, with small yards in front.

The plan of Cincinnati is similar to that of Philadelphia, and the streets are named in nearly the same way. It is well built, and said to be the most compact city in the United States. Its situation, on a natural plateau surrounded by an amphitheater of hills three hundred feet in height, with Covington and Newport, separated by the Licking River, on its southern half, and the resources of the entire Ohio River at its feet, is an enviable as well as a unique one. Nowhere are there such facilities for business, or such sites for handsome residences.

That Cincinnati is in great part a home for a large class of German-speaking people, is evident from the appellation of "Over the Rhine," belonging to that portion of the city separated from the main part by the Miami Canal, and seemingly a piece of the "Vaterland" set down in the midst of one of our most progressive American cities. Here, surrounded by a home-loving people, is the great Music Hall, justly the pride of the Queen City, with the handsome Exposition buildings, due also in a degree to these German citizens, whose love for music demanded a proper hall in which to hold their "Sängerfest." Over eight thousand people fill this great auditorium every two years, to hear the best orchestral and vocal music in the world, and in every part of the United States the Cincinnati Musical Festivals are treats to look forward to and be proud of. In this, the centennial year of the Ohio Valley, the city will be crowded to its utmost capacity.

To make the plan of Cincinnati definite, to turn back for a moment that we may present it as it is to eyes that have never seen it, is a difficult problem to work out in a necessarily limited space, where words are used to construct a sketch which appeals to the mind's vision. Yet to leave this unattempted would be unjust to the Cincinnati which crowns the chain of hills encircling the city proper; for in these linked heights we find a singularly perfect exhibit of the peculiar characteristics which define and illustrate the RIVER.

From where Mt. Adams juts out into the broken cliffs which

edge the river and overlook the crescent-shaped valley and the distant hills inclosing the twin cities that lie along the curving edge of the Kentucky shore, and from where its rugged flanks push backward into the chain, a continuous succession of swelling ridges environ the Cincinnati of trade, which is half hidden in the dense smoke that shrouds its countless industries. This sweep of the circling heights goes backward and onward, broken only by the deep and narrow valley of Deer Creek, and the wider valley of Mill Creek, which divides the steeps of Clifton from the bold escarpment of Price Hill, where the chain once more touches the river. This environment of hills for many years formed a barrier to the city's growth on the eastern, northern, and western sides. Villages and farm-houses found place here and there upon the summits, and vineyards covered the slopes that were not too steep to till. As soon as the advantages of their higher situation began to be appreciated, their growth increased with the multiplied and improved modes of travel to and from the city. The ravines which formed dividing lines have been filled up or bridged over, and the village names now serve to denote different localities of a breezy hilltop city of homes. To-day the inclined-planes and cable and electric railways carry many thousands of people up the heights, and the quondam rural villages are now the crown-jewels of the Queen City.

Beginning with the first point in the eastern chain of hills just sketched in outline, we return to MT. ADAMS. This was the site of the first Cincinnati Observatory, and here, in 1843, the corner-stone of that building was laid by ex-President John Quincy Adams. The observatory was managed by the Cincinnati Astronomical Society until 1872, when it became a department of the Cincinnati University, and was removed to its new building on Mt. Lookout.

From Mt. Adams, through Eden Park, where are the Art Museum and Art School buildings, substantially built of stone, we come to the residence portion of WALNUT HILLS. The Rev. James Kemper, a Presbyterian minister, who, in 1791, descended the river in a flat-boat, settled on the bold uplands north-east of the village of Cincinnati, and built a strong block-house, which was the only secure parsonage at that date.

The quaint old residence, remodeled from the original structure, still stands, but the lane, which once led down the hill, is now a well-paved street, lined with comfortable homes, and the Kemper lands are covered with a populous part of the suburban city, which still recalls, in name, its groves of native growth.

WALNUT HILLS is called the "Suburb of Churches," from the number and elegance of these edifices. This locality is the site of well-known rural homes, set in beautiful parks, where the changing vistas give charming river views.

AVONDALE, which adjoins Clifton and Walnut Hills, was until recently a model village, with its town hall and village school, its country roads and its shady lanes. Now the cable, electric, and steam railways seem to bring it much nearer the city; new streets are opening in all directions, and the work of building is busily going on.

MT. AUBURN, formerly called Keys's Hill, was early popular as a place of residence, and is now more closely built up than the other hill-top suburbs. The Cincinnati Orphan Asylum and the German Protestant Orphan Asylum are both situated here, and, like Walnut Hills and Avondale, Mt. Auburn boasts the presence of excellent educational institutions, both public and private.

CLIFTON surpasses all the other suburbs in the number and elegance of its residences and the beauty of its streets. Like Avondale, it is a separate incorporated village, and its citizens and municipality take pride in working for its welfare and improvement. No shops or factories are found within its limits, and the twenty miles of tree-lined avenues which wend their way between the spacious private estates, unmarred by fence or boundary-wall, unite to form a vast cultivated park. Clifton has a handsome town hall and public-school building, known as "Resor Academy" in front of which stands the beautiful fountain, the recent gift of Mr. Henry Probasco.

BURNET WOODS PARK, the old beech-forest, whose natural beauty has not been marred by artificial means, stands on the southern boundary of Clifton. Near it is the Zoological Garden, which contains over sixty acres of beautiful park, substantial buildings, and a fine collection of four-footed wild animals, birds, and reptiles, which is well worth seeing.

To the west of the city, and across Mill Creek, whose valley separates it from the northern hills, another ridge rises precipitously to the height of four hundred feet above the river-bed. Its summit, which is known as PRICE HILL, is reached by an inclined-plane railway and by the winding Warsaw pike. Here again are magnificent views of the city, river, and surrounding country. Price Hill has many handsome residences, comfortable homes, and numerous churches and schools.

On the Kentucky shore, opposite Price Hill, the highlands that inclose COVINGTON and NEWPORT fall in broken hill-terraces to the river; for at Ludlow is the south-east end of the encircling ridge, which crosses the Licking and sweeps around the wide extent of lowlands upon which the river plats of the

Kentucky towns were originally made. But the twin cities have broken their old boundaries. Houses are scattered in neighborly groups along the choice spots of the beautiful Covington highlands, and Newport has its secluded mansions that look down upon the Ohio River.

Above and below the cities the river on each side is lined with growing colonies of prosperous village suburbs, into which street railways are venturing, and thus the city links are being welded.

Several bridges cross the Ohio here. The suspension bridge, connecting Cincinnati with Covington, is a magnificent structure, erected at a cost of $1,800,000, and was opened in 1867.

As a work of art the bronze fountain, which has given its name to the square in the center of Cincinnati, stands among the finest in the United States, and was presented to the people in 1871 by Mr. Henry Probasco, as a memorial of his brother-in-law, the late Mr. Tyler Davidson. The bronze work is cast from cannon purchased of the Danish government; but the figures are in themselves a study, symbolizing the uses and blessings of water, by August von Kreling, the son-in-law of Kaulbach, and were carefully carried out in every detail by Herr von Müller, of Munich, Bavaria.

The Public Library, a handsome building on Vine Street, between Sixth and Seventh Streets, contains about seventy-two thousand volumes, and has been open to the public since 1874. The new Chamber of Commerce building, at Fourth and Vine Streets, is the work of the well-known architect, Richardson, and promises to take the first place among the city's handsome buildings, though the post-office and government offices occupy a very imposing one on Fountain Square, and most of the club-houses show remarkable architectural taste.

It is impossible in this short summary of Cincinnati to do justice to the city, its well-kept streets and watchful municipal government, and its progress in every particular. Its street-car system and fire department can not be excelled in any city in the United States; it contains many handsome churches, and is foremost in public charities; its educational facilities, in all branches of art and science, are unlimited.

In all mention of Cincinnati, its suburbs and the Kentucky cities of Covington and Newport are included, for though both of these cities across the river have important iron interests, and together about seventy thousand inhabitants, yet it is easy to see that the prosperity of the Queen City is theirs also, and that their fortunes are indissolubly connected.

A peculiarity of the Kentucky shore below Cincinnati is the curious composite rock formation, apparently washed here and there into hollows by the water. The Big Miami River empties into the Ohio nineteen miles below Cincinnati, between the States of Indiana and Ohio, and a short distance from the city of Lawrenceburg, Indiana, situated on what is known as the high bottom-lands, and an important manufacturing center. Lawrenceburg is a well-built town, supplied with a levee sufficient to preserve it from the highest floods.

A little farther down we pass Aurora, a growing city. Then several small ports, including Carrollton, Kentucky, one of the oldest settlements; Preston, Milton; and, on the right bank, Madison, Indiana, beautifully situated in the midst of a fertile valley. Bethlehem, Westport, Herculaneum, and Utica are passed in turn before reaching the Falls of the Ohio and the beautiful city stretching along the shore. The unusual importance of a location at the "Falls of the Ohio" was seized upon with a prophetic instinct by a small company of adventurous volunteers, who landed at the mouth of Bear Grass Creek on July 8, 1773, and these few men were the first elements of population, where to-day there is a great and wealthy city. Captain Bullitt, the head of this small company, laid out a town site, and the year following built a house; but it was not until three years later that the State of Kentucky was created a sovereign State. Gratitude to the French king, Louis XVI, for declaring against England in the War of the Revolution, suggested the name of Louisville, and there were probably nearly 1,000 inhabitants here and in the immediate vicinity in 1800. When the town was founded, the enormous value of a canal around the Falls had been considered; for it is certain that a map of the town, drawn in 1793, presented the projected canal virtually as it was built thirty-seven years later. If a history of the people of Louisville were written, it would comprise three distinct periods. The first would be the pioneer period; the second the building of the canal; and the third period "would comprise that of the organic change after the war, when the building of railroads, the abolition of slavery, and the development of agriculture in the new North-west temporarily endangered the future of the city."

The opening of new lines of railroads, and her connection with thirty-two navigable rivers, brings the Eastern coal-field, which covers one-fourth of the State's area, so near Louisville that it has had the effect of making coal for fuel cheaper here than anywhere else in the country. Coexistent with these coal-fields are forests of the finest timber known to the market. The virgin forest of Eastern Kentucky covers ten thousand square miles, and the Southern and Western forests are equally valuable and extensive. Louisville is now the best and cheapest hard-wood lumber market in the world, and in addition is the natural gateway to the celebrated Blue Grass region.

An account of the city of Louisville, however short, would be incomplete without at least a mention of its beautiful Public Library, containing more than 40,000 volumes, its educational institutions, and its numerous public and religious charities. There are four well-known medical institutions, the Kentucky Institutions for the white and colored blind, with the government printing establishment for the blind attached, and the Southern Baptist Theological Seminary. The public almshouse cost $210,000; and a unique charity is the Masonic Widows' and Orphans' Home, the single charity of the kind in the United States, and celebrated all over the world among Masons.

Louisville has six hospitals, eleven orphanages, two homes for friendless women, a home for old ladies, and a central organized charity association; also the best training-school for nurses in the country, with every facility and all expenses paid.

The city is also justly celebrated for its beautiful churches and Cave Hill Cemetery, of which the location is unrivaled.

Main Street still contains evidences of the original character of the city in some of the old business houses, and the river front, now in a continual turmoil of business and traffic, is the oldest quarter.

From the wharves three bridges span the Ohio, connecting with Louisville the cities of New Albany and Jeffersonville, Indiana, and opening the way for northern travel and traffic to the farther South through this thriving city. The one called the "Short Route," crossing the river below the Falls, connects the suburb of Portland with New Albany, Indiana, and is considered an engineering marvel. "Its lower end connects with the Kentucky and Indiana steel cantilever bridge. This beautiful structure, which cost $1,500,000, was begun in 1882, and completed in 1886. Its length is 2,453 feet, exclusive of the approaches, which, on the Kentucky side, are very picturesque and extensive. There are 9 piers, 7 of which are of limestone masonry, and 2 are cone-shaped iron cylinders, made of boiler-iron five-eighths of an inch thick, resting upon the bed-rock, and fitted with brick and concrete. The average height of the piers is 170 feet. The masonry of these piers is regarded by engineers as the most handsome and substantial ever placed in position for a bridge on the continent. The aggregate masonry contains 13,600 cubic yards of stone. The length of approaches on the Indiana side is 781 feet, and on the Kentucky side 3,990 feet. The bridge contains 2,414,261 pounds of steel and 3,625,000 pounds of wrought iron. It affords accommodation for railway, carriage, street-car, and foot traffic.

New Albany and Jeffersonville are practically a part of Louisville. New Albany is the county-seat of Floyd County. It is located in the center of the Ohio valley, three miles below the Falls of the Ohio River, opposite the city of Louisville, Kentucky, in latitude 38° 18' north, and longitude 8° 49' west. It is laid out upon an elevated plateau, upon two benches or plains, one twenty feet higher than the other, and sweeping northward and westward to a range of hills, that bear from the Indians the poetic name of the "Silver Hills," and which are from three hundred to five hundred feet in height. These hills, in the vicinity of the city, are being covered with charming suburban residences, many of them of beautiful architecture in design and adornment. The city was laid out in 1813 by Joel, Abner, and Nathaniel Scribner, the original plat embracing but eight hundred and twenty-six acres, the land being entered at the government land-office at Vincennes, when that town was the capital of the Territory of Indiana, and purchased by the Scribners. The lots were disposed of by public auction on the first Tuesday and Wednesday of November, 1813, and the proprietors of the town stipulated that "one-fourth part of each payment upon lots sold shall be paid into the hands of trustees, to be chosen by the purchasers, until such payments shall amount to $5,000, the interest of which is to be applied to the support of schools in the town for the use of its inhabitants forever." New Albany was incorporated as a city in July, 1839, having a population of four thousand two hundred.

From the river, Louisville, with its pretty suburbs, Parkland, Clifton, "The Highlands," Anchorage, and Pewee Valley, makes a striking picture, supplemented by the famous Indiana "Knobs," which cross the Ohio below New Albany.

Clarksville, Indiana, evidently the site of an Indian village, and Shippenport, Kentucky (Shippingport), incorporated in 1785 as Campbelltown, are both swallowed up in the growth of Louisville, and long ago incorporated with the city. Shippenport in 1815 was made of importance by the French, who erected there an enormous flouring-mill, which now stands, converted into a cement-factory.

The Louisville and Portland Canal "was opened in 1831, and was the first great engineering work in the United States; it proved eventually too small to accommodate all the craft on the Ohio, and the work of deepening and widening it was begun in 1860. The improvement was continued through the war up to 1866, when it ceased for lack of appropriations. In 1868 Congress voted $300,000 for resuming the abandoned work, and followed it by $300,000 more in 1869, and $300,000 in 1871, and gave $100,000 in 1873. Having thus expended such large sums, the next natural step was for the government to assume entire charge of the canal, which was accomplished in 1874 by the United States assuming the payment of outstanding bonds. From the date of the transfer, all forms of toll charges were abolished, and to this fact the waning powers of river transportation owe whatever vitality remains at the present time.

"Under government auspices and direction the task of completing the enlargement of the canal has not only been carried to completion, but a new project is now under way to successful accomplishment by which a secure and ample harbor will be afforded against the perils of moving ice in the colder seasons, for those large fleets of coal-tows that arrive from Pittsburgh with high stages of water. All the property is under responsible supervision by officers of the government, and the canal proper, with the improvements projected, will long remain as sightly memorials of a government devoted to the interests of inter-State commerce."

Below the Falls, near the village of Clarksville, there is a strong whirlpool through which, however, steamers can pass without danger. Perhaps the Ohio River is more beautiful at this point than anywhere from Pittsburgh to Cairo, broken at every mile with small islands, and on both sides shut in by long ranges of hills changing in shape with every turn and bend of the rippling water. The small towns of West Point and Brandenburg, Kentucky, and Mauckport and Leavenworth, Indiana, in the vicinity of the Wyandot Cave, may be mentioned; then Alton, Indiana; Concordia, Kentucky; Rome, Indiana; and Stephensport, with Hawesville, Kentucky, opposite Cannelton, where there is drab and reddish sandstone, that is useful for subterranean and subaqueous work, such as foundation walls and bridge piers and abutments; and Tell City, Indiana; Lewisport, Kentucky; Grand View and Rockport, Indiana; and 149 miles below Louisville is Owensboro, Kentucky, the county-seat of Daviess County.

One hundred and eighty-three miles below Louisville we reach Evansville, Indiana, situated on a high bluff, always above high-water mark. It is also situated at the head of low-water navigation, midway between the Falls of the Ohio and its mouth. It is nine miles below the mouth of Green River, which drains that marvelously rich valley; 40 miles above the Wabash River, a noble tributary of the Ohio, flowing through the most fruitful grain-producing country in the West; it is 140 miles above the mouth of the Cumberland, and 150 miles above the mouth of the Tennessee, the two magnificent streams that form the water-way of the iron and coal regions of Tennessee and Alabama.

Evansville is now, and has always been, the entrepôt for all these rivers, her steamboat lines having grown in number and wealth until they have practically a monopoly of the entire carrying trade of these streams.

Evansville was named for General Robert M. Evans, born in Virginia in 1783, and died in 1844. He was an aid-de-camp of General Harrison, and led a portion of his brigade in the famous battle of Tippecanoe. Its large temperance hall was built mainly at the suggestion of his daughter-in-law, Mrs. Selita Evans, in the town that bears his name.

A mile below Evansville is Lamasco, and twelve miles below is Henderson, Kentucky, which is said to be the richest town of its size in the country. A magnificent railroad bridge spans the Ohio River at Henderson, being the longest that crosses the river, and having cost $2,000,000.

The Kentucky shore now becomes very bare except for innumerable small landings. On the Indiana shore, after West Franklin, comes the town of Mount Vernon. Then the river is everywhere broken by little islands; and twelve miles below Uniontown the Wabash divides the State of Indiana from Illinois. Raleigh is opposite.

Shawneetown, an old site and a prosperous town, follows in Illinois; Caseyville and Weston, in Kentucky ; 860 miles below Pittsburgh is the famous Cave in Rock, Illinois, noted for its great natural beauty, and as wild a spot as there is on the whole Ohio River. For years it was the rendezvous of a daring gang of outlaws, known as Murrell's men.

Separated by only two or three miles from each other are Elizabethtown, Rose Clare, and Golconda, Illinois; and a little above Smithland, Kentucky, the Cumberland River empties into the Ohio. Paducah, twelve miles below, is at the mouth of the Tennessee River. Below Paducah there are the towns of Brooklyn, Belgrade, Metropolis, Caledonia, and Mound City, Illinois, a city of "great expectations," which have never yet been realized. Its situation is most favorable for manufacturing, and the deep water from here all the way down to Cairo makes it the best winter harbor for vessels in Western waters. The prosperity or decay of the city—its destiny, in fact—is bound up in that of Cairo. It was an important naval station during the war.

Thus approaching the city of Cairo, Illinois, one can not fail to realize its wonderful position at the junction of the Ohio and Mississippi Rivers. Though in 1842 only 60 of the

2,000 enterprising people were left, on account of financial disaster, who in 1841 came here to found a town, yet the active, prosperous city of to-day shows no trace of any ill-fortune. From a first glance one would suppose the situation unsafe, on account of the frequent floods of the two rivers; but examination shows the city to be well guarded by immense levees, which are only needed to protect it from overflow during one or two months in the year; during the remaining ten or eleven it is far above the level of

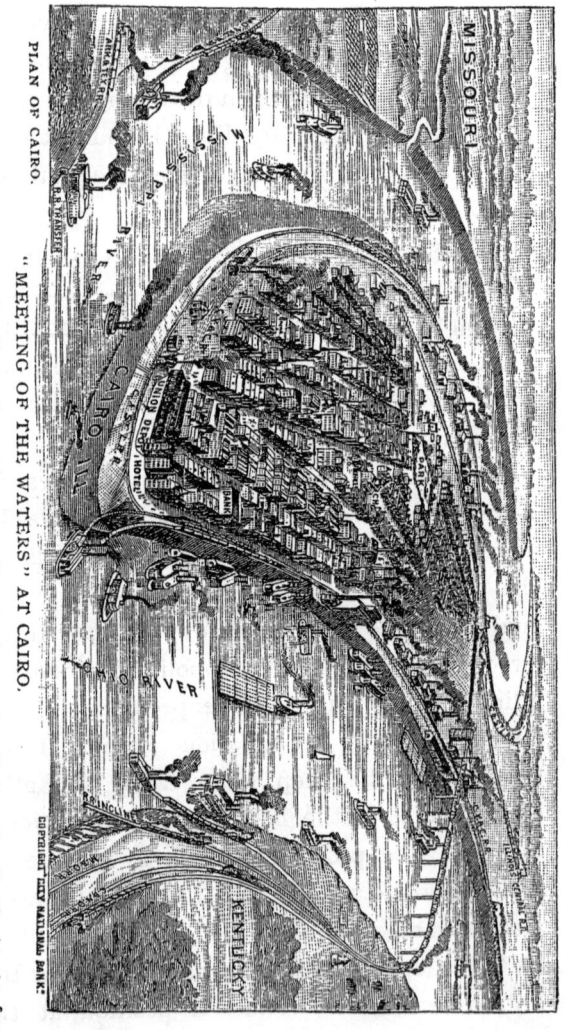

the waters, and the system of drainage is perfect. Cairo is the gateway to the entire South.

No richer soil than that of Cairo and Alexander County can be found anywhere. The products of the North, the South, the East, and the West are produced at their very doors. Corn, that great Northern product, is produced more abundantly here than anywhere else in the country. The flour manufactured from the white winter wheat commands the highest price in the markets of the world. Oats are produced with profit everywhere here, while sorghum-cane, Irish and sweet potatoes, and all ordinary farm products grow in the greatest profusion. Western Kentucky is admirably adapted to the growth of tobacco, while it is raised abundantly in Southern Illinois, especially in Williamson County, and also in South-east Missouri. Fields of growing cotton, that great Southern staple, may be seen blooming every year within thirty miles of the city, in South-east Missouri. Clover seems to be indigenous in all this part of the country, and its production, both for hay and for the seed, is increasing rapidly.

All the uplands of Southern Illinois, Western Kentucky, and South-eastern Missouri are pre-eminently adapted to the raising of fruits and vegetables. Large fields are devoted to pie-plant and tomatoes. Strawberry-fields, ranging in size from one to forty acres, are found here. The crop is never a failure, and is generally profitable. Raspberries, blackberries, and all the smaller fruits grow luxuriantly. The crop of blackberries, which grow wild in the woods in all this part of the country, is beyond measure. A plain statement of the facts would seem almost incredible.

The culture of grapes upon the hillsides of Pulaski County is a growing industry, and is found to be very profitable. Apples and pears are produced for market, and with profit, while peaches are successfully raised about thirteen to fourteen years out of twenty. The demand for peaches is such that an orchard bearing a good peach-crop once in three years is a valuable investment. Just across the river, in Missouri, in the counties of Mississippi and Scott, there is a large area of country, embracing many thousands of acres of the finest land, which seems especially adapted to the raising of watermelons.

In seasons of great plenty, fruit here frequently rots on the ground, when, as often happens, the market is overcrowded, as Cairo is the center of the best fruit-growing region between New Jersey and Southern California.

It is said by experts that Cairo is the most convenient point in the country for the manufacture of iron and steel. A mixture of ores is always necessary for this purpose, and the cost of transportation, an important item; and nowhere can coal, limestone, and coke be brought together so cheaply as at Cairo. Fine Bessemer steel could be produced here at less cost than at any other point in the United States. These facts were recognized by a Pittsburgh iron king, but he died before the erection of his contemplated iron-works here could be carried out, and it remains for some one else to execute his unfinished plans.

We have now floated the entire length of this wonderful river. Touching its commercial and industrial importance to the Republic, the following cutting may not be inappropriate: "The seven States lying contiguous to the Ohio River, whose resources make up the vast wealth of the Ohio Valley, have within half a million of the population of the Atlantic States. The tonnage and commerce of the Ohio River is equal in value to the import and export tonnage of the entire Atlantic sea-board. The Ohio River States have paid in internal revenue taxes over

$100,000,000 since 1861, and yet millions are spent on improvements along the sea-coast, where only hundreds are spent in improving the Ohio River."

Before our last word is written, we wish to say to the reader who has come with us thus far, that the unsketched Ohio, which we have not been able to present to you "in its very habit as it lives," is as charming and attractive as are many of the pictured pages we have laid before you. Some of the un-illustrated rivers—for the affluents that feed it are a part of itself—have not the grandeur, nor the weird fascination of the mountain views of its Allegheny-born streams; yet there is nothing more unique in lowland, sylvan scenery than the luxuriant vegetation which covers the valleys of the Muskingum, the Hocking, the Scioto, the Miamis, and the Wabash Rivers. Above the rich bottom-lands rise low, rounded hills, that skirt the winding shores in a panoramic succession of changing vistas. The freshness and tenderness, the variety of scenery thus given to the long river-reaches, mocks the skill of the writer, while it yet courts the pencil of the artist.

And now for that "last word" which awaits the saying, and which is somewhat difficult to say. It is addressed to the dwellers by the RIVER; and to those who live upon, and gather their gains from its waters.

It was not without reason that the illustrations selected for this book were drawn chiefly from the mountain regions "WHERE THE RIVER IS BORN," and from the forest uplands, where, in the deep, cool, shaded pools, the pure life-giving and life-conserving waters are collected.

The pictured exhibit we have herein given of the unspoiled river, while it lingers in the thickly wooded retreats of the mountain glens, is of itself a plea for the preservation of its purity in the thousand-mile course it runs through the lowlands. If the lovers of the Ohio do not defend it from the evils civilization has begun to fasten, and will fasten upon it a hundred years from now, the beautiful valley of the " Deep Shining River " will be the valley of the shadow of Death.*

Nature, with her eternal resistance to man's misdoing, is constantly striving to free the river. The floods, with all their distructiveness, are not altogether evil besoms. Their rapid action has, time and again, started the sluggish currents between neighboring islands, and forced the quick motion of living waters into the forgotten by-paths of the stream. The STEAMBOATS also create a certain activity which assists in the release of obstructions; and the RIVER COMMISSION has been of immense use in keeping the channels open. But the factor which could do most, and which is doing least, is PUBLIC OPINION. Let that giant shoulder the cause of the river, and sanitary science will smilingly come forward with all the appliances of experience and skill, to forward the good work.

The retired steamboatmen, who are struggling to sustain the *ennui* of existence in the gloom-breeding grandeur of gilded *salons* (unlike, and not so heartsome as the "Ladies' Cabin"), should do something for the relief of the beautiful highway, of the waters, upon which they met benignant fortune. Their knowledge of the river, their experience of its moods, the concrete wisdom, with its resultant use, which is the informing

---

* The reader is assured that this is not merely an æsthetic point, used to win the sympathy of the lovers of the beautiful, but a question of grave and material importance to the dwellers in the towns and cities upon the RIVER. Should it serve for another quarter of a century as a great open sewer for dead animals, and an unlimited number of sewer systems; each lovely winding river-stretch will be a central curve from which malarial evolvents will be described, the locus of the centers of hundreds of deadly circles.

Thought of their collective accrescence, all warrant their fitness for the rôle of "advisory council" to the "River Legislators;" who now only add a "worse confounded confusion" to the hopeless entanglements of the "How Not To Do It" Bureau, of Internal Improvements at Washington.

The Inter-state Law did awaken a rippling ebb and flow of trade upon the river; and if the "Line" autocrats and the "Old-timers" will "pull together" the trade will swell into an "Ohio flood." For a well-ordered "Line" of "Passenger and Light Freight Steamers," running as DAY-BOATS, connecting at proper distances from Pittsburgh to Cairo, would open the river to a new traveling public. Tourists, lovers of beautiful scenery, people who travel for pleasure and who take pleasure in travel, would seek the luxurious motion and the lovely outlook, to be found under a canvas awning, in a reclining-chair, upon the "hurricane-deck" of a light-draught "side-wheeler" in MID-RIVER.

APPENDIX.

APPENDIX A, No. I.—PAGE 42.

THE fact here admitted, that "*these people had lived with La Salle for some months*," refutes the statement made immediately after by M. Gallinée, that "La Salle did not understand the Iroquois language." To accent properly the contradictory "fact" and "statement," an excerpt from the records is added. "If M. de la Salle had not preferred glory to gain, he had only to stay quietly in his fort and accumulate at least twenty-five thousand livres a year through the trade that he had drawn there. One can say with truth that he is the only man who could conduct the enterprise with which he has been charged. He is irreproachable in manners, discreet in his conduct, and he maintains order among his people. . . . He understands civil, military, and naval architecture; he is a good agriculturist; he speaks or understands four or five of the Indian dialects, and has a great facility for acquiring languages; he knows Indian customs and manners, and turns them as he will through his address and eloquence, as well as through their esteem for him. In his journeys he lives no better than his people, and is willing to suffer any hardship to encourage them, and there is reason to believe that with the protection of the ministries he will found colonies of more value to France than any that have yet been established."

APPENDIX A, No. II.—PAGE 53.

THE original Ohio Company was organized to secure to the English the Ohio, and to check the progress southward of the "New France," apparently so firmly planted in Canada, by establishing trading-posts, protected by small forts west of the Alleghenies. In 1848, a petition to the crown was sent over, in which Thomas Lee, Lawrence and Augustus Washington, Robert Dinwiddie, surveyor-general for the Southern Colonies, and their associates, among whom was John Hanbury—an influential citizen, as well as a leading merchant of London—asked for a grant of "500,000 acres of land between the Monongahela and the Kanawha, or on the northern margin of the Ohio." In March, 1749, the king instructed the governor of Virginia, to whom all this vast territory belonged, to make the grant. Before 1748, when the Ohio Company was formed, there were no settlements west of the mountains.

Hitherto the Indian trade had been, so far as the English were concerned, almost entirely confined to Western Pennsylvania. For, owing to the constant and relentless conflicts between the Indians and the early settlers in Kentucky, trade there meant the spoil of the victor.

The original "Ohio Company" won favor with influential personages in England and in all the Southern Colonies, yet the constant troubles in which the whole country was involved retarded its progress. Its one great success was the promotion of emigration westward, and the stability of the settlements effected by its efforts; which, although interrupted by the condition of affairs, were constantly resumed, until the success of the Revolution rendered its existence unnecessary.

As early as 1751 their agent visited the tribes upon the Great Miami River, and established a trading-post in one of the Twigtwee towns, belonging to the Miami Confederacy. The trail opened by this trade was from the Miami towns to the mouth of the Scioto, down the Ohio to the Falls, and back by way of the Kentucky River and the Cumberland Gap to Virginia, which was then much the safest route, as the Southern Indians were less inimical to the English than were the Lake tribes.

In 1760, nearly a century after the discovery of the Ohio by La Salle, the Virginia "Ohio Company" resumed the surveys which were interrupted by the French and English war.

One singular fact connected with the history of the time deserves notice: "Mr. Lawrence Washington, upon whom fell the chief management of the affairs of this company after the death of Mr. Lee, conceived the very plausible plan of inviting the "Pennsylvania Dutch" and their brethren from Germany to colonize this region. Their only objection was the *parish taxes* they would have to pay to support the Episcopal Church. Mr. Washington exerted himself to get this difficulty removed, but High Church Episcopacy was too strong for him, and so his scheme failed; and a large portion of Western Pennsylvania and Virginia was kept open for a different race—mainly for Scotch-Irish Presbyterians. . . . Mr. Washington, in a letter to Mr. Hanbury, of London, wrote: 'I conversed with all the Pennsyvania Dutch whom I met, and much recommended their settling. The chief reason against it was the payment of an English clergyman, whom few understood, while none made use of him. It has been my opinion, and I hope ever will be, that restraints on conscience are cruel in regard to those on whom they are imposed, and injurious to the country imposing them. . . . As the ministry have thus far shown the true spirit of patriotism by encouraging the extending of our dominions in America, I doubt not, by an application, they would go still further and complete what they have begun, by procuring some kind of charter to prevent the residents on the Ohio and its branches from being subject to parish taxes. They all assured me that they might have from Germany any number of settlers, could they but obtain their favorite exemption. I have promised to endeavor for it, and now do my utmost by this letter.' " (History of "The Old Redstone Presbytery.")

APPENDIX A, No. III.—PAGE 64.

In 1774 the first Continental Congress, in its second session, had appointed commissioners to reoccupy Fort Pitt, and make treaties with the Indians on behalf of the new government. The British had garrisons in the Lake forts. In Kentucky, Walker, Boone, Bullit, Kenton, Harrod, the McAfees, the Taylors, and others, were building stockades for defense against the Indians, who were supplied with arms and ammunition by the English.

The master-spirit of the time, George Rogers Clark, of Albemarle County, Virginia, was in Philadelphia perfecting his plans for an offensive campaign into the Illinois country, which was to overawe the disaffected tribes, and win the wavering for the new government. On the 2d of June, 1774, the British Parliament had passed an act which included in the bounds of Canada all the country between the Ohio River and the Lakes. It had already become evident that it was to be defended by their Indian allies. Clark secured the cordial co-operation of Patrick Henry, then governor of Virginia. After many vexatious delays this force was finally assembled at Fort Pitt, and went down the Ohio, arriving at Louisville the 24th of June, 1778, where he was joined by the Kentucky volunteers. On the 4th of July they entered Kaskaskia after nightfall, and the first intimation the inhabitants had of their presence was the startling cry, "If any one comes into the streets he shall be shot."

On the 6th of February, 1778, France had recognized the independence of the United States. Clark heard the news on the Mississippi, and immediately began recruiting a company made up of the French settlers, and through them influenced the Indians to make common cause with the Long Knives and the French against the English. Through Grand Door, the leading chief of the Piankeshaws, this was accomplished. The news spread through the Illinois tribes. A council of representative chiefs met at Kahokia, and the alliance Clark proposed was ratified.

Captain Helm, with a fighting contingent of *one* soldier, represented the Americans at Vincennes when it was captured by a force of nearly five hundred British and Indians. Helm had ordered a "halt" when they were within hearing distance, and Colonel Hamilton stopped, but demanded the surrender of the garrison. "On what terms?" asked Helm. "The honors of war," replied Hamilton. And on those terms Vincennes was surrendered.

A Spanish trader, named Francis Vigo, carried the news to Clark, who decided at once to recapture the place, and with sturdy determination and daring started across the flooded country in February. When they approached the Wabash it took three days wading through the flooded shallows to gain the bank. Again there were flooded wastes to cross before reaching the town.

On the 24th Hamilton surrendered Vincennes, and the entire Northwest, except the Lake posts, was held by the Americans. A convoy of stores and provisions on its way from Detroit to the British at Vincennes was captured a few days after the surrender by Captain Helm, who was released at the capitulation. Hamilton was sent a prisoner to Virginia, where he was put in irons and treated with great severity for having offered the Indians premiums for "white scalps."

Among the great leaders of the pioneers, the men who marched in the forefront of battle and of civilization, there is no more martial figure than that of George Rogers Clark. He was one of those "born fighters" who always reach their place in the world at the opportune moment. Because of his Virginian birth he was all the more the Kentuckian of the Kentuckians. In the logic of that time a war of defense was a war of extermination, and raids into the Indian country were always raids of reprisal. Such a fighter "cared little for gain, and still less for his hide;" but Dame Fortune, who loves men of his mettle, kept putting into his hands the forsaken opportunities and the dropped threads of less lucky adventurers. But one man has ever stood above Clark in the estimation of the State and the hearts of the people; and to be *second* to that man was a patent of princely rank; for HENRY CLAY was the flower of his race, and the uncrowned king of Kentucky.

APPENDIX A, No. IV.—PAGE 65.

SETTLEMENT OF GALLIPOLIS.

IN 1791 a French colony settled at Gallipolis. It was largely made up of the better middle class, anxious to escape the opening horrors of the French Revolution. They had purchased lands of "The Scioto Company," which Judge Hall says, in his "Statistics of the West," "was formed from, or was an offshoot of, the Ohio Company.

"This company should not be confounded with the original 'Ohio Company,' organized by the Washingtons, the Lees, other Maryland and Virginia gentlemen, and the Hanburys of London in, 1748. The original Ohio Company, after having achieved the objects for which they were organized, the settlement of families upon the lands granted them by the king, and 'the establishment of trading-posts and frontier-posts to protect these settlers from the French and the Indians,' had dissolved, and left the unoccupied lands free to all comers. The new 'Ohio Company,' organized by the Putnams and other New Englanders in 1786, took the title of the old company, without any distinguishing prefix to show that there was not the slightest connection or interest which warranted the revival of the name."

"The Scioto Company," a branch of the new "Ohio Company," sent in June of 1788, one Joel Barlow to France to distribute "Proposals to Colonists," and sell them lands.

We give a quotation from their "Proposals," which is, of itself, evidence of the intended fraud:

"The climate is wholesome and delightful. Frost, even in winter, is almost entirely unknown. A river called, for its eminence, 'The Beautiful River,' abounds in excellent fish of vast size. There are noble forests, consisting of trees that *spontaneously produce sugar*, and *a plant that yields ready-made candles.* There is venison in plenty; no dangerous wild animals, but swine which multiply from a pair to two hundred in two or three years without the trouble or expense of caring for them. There are no taxes and no military service." Howe, from whom we are quoting, continues: "A handsomely engraved colored map represented the Scioto Company's tract as extending one hundred miles north of the mouth of the Kanawha. The lands of the Ohio Company to the east, next to which was the plat of an inhabited and cleared country, had upon the plat these words: '*Sept rangs de municipalité acquis par des individues et occupés depuis,* 1786.' The map is as inaccurate in geography as it is fraudulent in its statements, for it represents the country as cleared and inhabited, when it was, in fact, a wilderness."

The agent seems to have happily timed his enterprise. The darkest days of the French Revolution were dawning, and doubtful of what would be the ending, people caught at this offer of an unoccupied paradise. Deeds were executed and recorded at Paris, and five hundred victims of the fraud—*for there was neither grant nor tract, no Scioto Company legally existing*—sailed for America, landing at Alexandria. There had been partial arrangements made for the reception of the emigrants from France before they left France. The first town planned, "Fair Haven," was so unfair a haven that it was submerged as soon it was laid out; then "Colonel Rufus Putnam made a clearing and erected block-houses and cabins at Gallipolis, four miles below, which was ten feet above high-water mark." Among the five hundred who came to Gallipolis there were twelve farmers and laborers. After six months the "company," which had agreed to supply provisions, stopped the supply. The only excuse given was that "their agent in France had run away with the money paid for the lands."

The winter was unusually severe, and the Kanawha and the Ohio were frozen over. The hunters brought no meat, and the colonists had no flour. The "Ohio Company" disavowed the sales, and the poor, deluded French people learned from the Indians that the pretended "Scioto Company" was composed of "New Englanders who resided at a great distance from Gallipolis. Their names even were unknown to the French, who spoke no English." After suffering the extreme of want, many died of the privations and the heart-breaking disappointment. A swamp in the rear of the village caused a frightful epidemic, and, although a French lawyer living in Philadelphia finally got them a special grant from the government, very few of the five hundred colonists brought from France settled on these lands.

APPENDIX A, No. V.—PAGE 182.

The Iroquois Indians, who guided La Salle to the Falls of the OHIO, borrowed the name which they gave the RIVER from the Delaware language. In the varied dialects of the Confederation it was indifferently called Ohio or Allegheny, both signifying "fine," "fair," or "shining river." In the Canadian Records it is given, "*Ohio ou Olighisipon que veut dire en Iroquois et en Outaouac La Belle Rivière.*" [Ohio or Olighisipon which, in the Iroquois and Ottawa language, means The Beautiful River.] However, in the different dialects, the name was so changed by elisions and additions that the original meaning is but imperfectly preserved.

Among the varied names we find "OHIOPÉCHEN," "OHIOPHANNE," "OHIOPÉCKHANNE;" and by different translators the names are given as "VERY WHITE STREAM," "VERY DEEP WHITE RIVER," "THE SHINING RIVER," "THE WHITE SHINING RIVER," and "THE DEEP BROKEN SHINING RIVER." The last gives a key to the meaning, as it was evidently suggested by the wind-capped undulations in the long river-reaches; particularly is this noticeable in the wide stretches between low-lying shores, after the large Southern affluents have poured in the waters they collected in the Allegheny and Cumberland Mountains. Besides, the reader should not forget that, through its northern and southern affluents conjoined, the Ohio drains an area of 190,464 square miles.

Before closing this last page the Editor wishes to give such brief mention as the space permits, to authors and authorities that have been particularly helpful in this work. First, to M. MARGRY; for only since the publication of the records in the French Archives could the outline history of the Discoverer and the Discovery of the Ohio be given as authentic beyond cavil. Before that valuable work was given to the public—*Découvertes et Établissements des Français dans l'Amérique Septentrionale, par Pierre Margry*—there were, here and there, brief allusions to the discoveries of LA SALLE in the writings of his contemporaries. But these were so uncertain in character, and apparently so unadvised in statement, that they seemed rather broken echoes running through the centuries—vague sounds suggestive of some hidden history—than definite or connected data upon which to found belief. Next to these records of the

238   *THE PICTURESQUE OHIO.*

Canadian Reports, nothing could have been more suggestive than PARK-
MAN'S admirably written Histories. From Parkman long extracts have
been given, which told the story of Pontiac so well that any change in the
wording would have been a loss to the reader. In addition to what is borrowed from these two unique authorities, the Editor wishes to acknowl-
edge an indebtedness for local coloring to JUDGE HALL, HOWE, and the
legion of writers who have sketched the salient points of Western adventures and adventurers.

C. M. C.

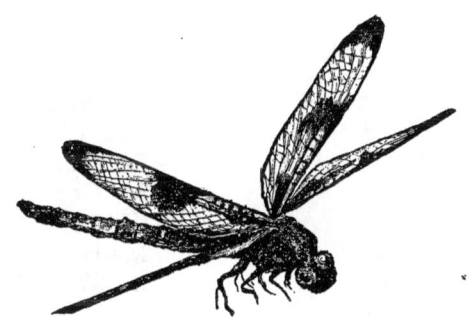

FULLNAME INDEX

ACKERMANN, K 13
ADAMS, 63 John 208 John Quincy 213
ALLOUEZ, 38
AMES, Fisher 97
AMHERST, Jeffrey 115
ARBUCKLE, Capt 141-142
ARMSTRONG, Capt 149
ASBURY, Francis 8
ASHLEY, Lt 81
AUBIN, Lt 117
BABY, M 125 130
BARLOW, Joel 235
BARTHELMY, M 41
BARTON, Capt 171
BAYARD, Stephen 194
BIGGS, John 81
BOONE, 7 233
BOSWELL, Col 177
BOUQUET, 109 Col 193
BOYD, Col 168 Ensign 154
BRADDOCK, 114 Gen 58
BRADY, 87-88 97 Samuel 86
BULLIT, 233
BULLITT, Capt 218 Thomas 63 205
BURBECK, Henry 155 Maj 154
BUTLER, Gen 150-152 Richard 150
CAMPAN, 134
CAMPBELL, John 193 Maj 120 123 125
CARPENTER, 77
CASS, Gen 180
CAVELIER, 38 Jean 35 Madame 36 Robert 34-35 37 39 Robert Rene 33
CHAPETON, 122
CHARLES, The Simple 34
CHRISTIAN, Col 138
CHRISTIE, Ensign 129-130
CLARK, 235 George Rogers 64 92-93 179 210 233-234
CLAVERHOUSE, 110
CLAY, Gen 176-179 Green 176 Henry 206 235

240   *THE PICTURESQUE OHIO.*

CLINTON, Dewitt 140
COLBERT, 34
COLE, S W 209
COLLINS, 92 Joel 91 93-95
   Judge 93 Mr 94 Mrs 94
   Stephen 90 93-94
COLUMBUS, 6-7
COMBS, Capt 176 Leslie
   176
CONTRECOEUR, 56
COOK, 172
CORNWALLIS, 145
CORTEZ, 38
CRAIG, Isaac 194 Neville B
   194
CRANSTON, 9
CRAWFORD, 90 Col 79-82
   84 John 81 William 79
   81-82
CRESAP, Col 136 141
CROGAN, George 54
CROGHAN, George 179
CROMWELL, 110 182
CURTS, 9
DALZELL, 133-134 Capt
   132
DAVIDSON, Tyler 216
DAVIES, 172 Maj 170-171
   Robert 121
DAVIESS, Maj 169
DECHANTAL, Jane 204
DECOURCELLES, M 40
DENNY, Maj 150-152
DEQUEYLUS, Abbe 39-41
DESEVIGNE, Madame 204
DESNOYERS, 121
DESOTO, 38
DEVILLIERS, 57

DINWIDDIE, Gov 54 57
   Robert 231
DODDRIDGE, 78
DOLLIER, M 39-42 44 48
DOUGHTY, Maj 148
DUBOIS, Capt 169-170 T
   169
DUDLEY, Col 177
DUNMORE, Gov 136 Lord
   97 136 138-140
DUQUESNE, Marquis 55
EVANS, Robert M 223 Selita
   223
FIELD, Col 137
FLEMING, Col 137 William
   137
FLOYD, Maj 166
FORBES, Joseph 59
FRANKLIN, 58
FROTHINGHAM, Lt 149
FRY, Col 56
FULTON, 211
GALLINEE, Abbe 41 48 M
   42 46 231
GAMELIN, Antoine 147 Mr
   148
GIBSON, John 140
GILMORE, 141-142
GIRTY, Mr 82 Simon 63 75
   82-84 111
GIST, Christopher 113
GLADWYN, 118-125 127-
   128 131-133 135 Maj
   115 117 130
GODEFROY, 122
GOUIN, M 117 123
GRANT, Capt 133-134
GRAVES, 175

INDEX

GREENE, Maj-gen 154
GUIGER, Capt 171
HALL, Capt 142 John 141
   Judge 235 238
HAMILTON, 141 Col 234
HAMTRAMCK, Maj 147-148
   150-151
HANBURY, 235 John 231
   Mr 233
HARDIN, Col 148-149
HARDING, Col 153
HARMAR, Gen 148-149
HARRISON, 171 173-175
   180 Benjamin 158 Capt
   160 Col 82 Gen 162
   175-176 178-181 223
   Gov 164-166 168 170 Lt
   159 Maj 81 W H 180
   William Henry 136 160
   172
HARROD, 233
HAY, Lt 132
HELM, Capt 234
HENRY, Patrick 233
HILDRETH, Dr 194
HODGDEN, Quartermaster-
   gen 150
HOLMES, Ensign 115 128
HOWE, 236 238
HULL, 174
INDIAN, Captain Pipe 82-83
   Catharine 117
   Cornplanter 153-154
   Cornstalk 139-142
   Elinipsico 142 Els-kwa-
   taw-a 162 Grand Door
   234 Little Turtle 95 147
   149 159 Logan 136

INDIAN (cont.)
   140-141
   Michilimackinac 113
   New Arrow 153 Nitarikyk
   39 Ol-li-wa-chi-ca 162
   Pipe 82 Pontiac 103-105
   108 113-125 131-132
   135 147 182 238
   Prophet 162 167 169-
   170 172-173 Redhawk
   141-142 Tanacharisen
   112 Tecumseh 162-167
   172-173 175 177-178
   181-182 White Eyes 139
   Wingenim 82
JACKSON, Stonewall 111
JACOBS, 135
JEFFERSON, 160 Mr 140
JENKINS, Lt 128
JOHNSON, Col 181 Richard
   M 181 William 108 193
JOLLIET, Sieur 48
KAULBACH, 216
KEMPER, James 214
KENTON, 233
KIRKLAND, Dr 97
KNIGHT, Dr 81
KNOX, Gen 156
LABROSSE, 127
LABUTTE, 119 122-123
LARRABEE, Lt 172
LASALLE, 7 33 35 39 41-42
   45 53 55 104-105 205
   232 237 Le Sieur De 50
   M De 34 40 44 47-49
   231
LEE, 112 204 235 Mr 232
   Thomas 53 231

LEFTWICH, Gen 175
LEWIS, Andrew 136 Charles 137 Col 137 Gen 137-139
LINN, Wm 93
LOGAN, Ben 93
LOUIS, XVI King Of France 218
LOWREY, Lt 154
LUDLOW, Denman 210 Israel 210
MADISON, President 172 174
MARGRY, M 49 Pierre 237
MARGY, M 237
MARQUETTE, 38
MARSHALL, Chief-justice 152
MASSIE, Henry 208
MATTHEWS, George 138
MAY, John 66
MCAFEE, 63 233
MCAFFEE, 169
MCARTHUR, Gen 180
MCCONNELL, Alec 92 Alexander 92
MCCOURN, 63
MCCULLOCH, John 76 Maj 75-76 Samuel 75-76
MCDOUGAL, Lt 123
MCKENDREE, Wm 8
MCKINLEY, John 82
MCKINNEY, 94 John 93 Wildcat 93-94
MICHAUX, 191
MILLS, Thomas 90
MONTCALM, 105
MONTROSE, 110

MOORE, Mr 98
MORGAN, 86 David 84 Gen 84 Mr 84-85 Stephen 84-85
MORRIS, Robert 98 158
MURRELL, 224
NEYON, M 125
NORDHOFF, Charles 200
OLDHAM, Col 150 152
OLIVER, William 176
OWEN, Col 171
PALMER, Andrew 54
PARKER, Thomas 208
PARKMAN, 238
PATOULET, 34
PATTERSON, Robert 210
PAULLY, 128 Ensign 127
PENN, J 194 J Jr 194
PERRY, 181 Commodore 180 Oliver Hazard 180
PITT, 59
PIZARRO, 38
POE, 97
POTHIER, Father 124
PRESTON, John 110
PRICE, Maj 157
PROBASCO, Henry 215
PROCTOR, 175 177-178 Gen 176 179
PUTNAM, Rufus 236
R, Col 97
RAPP, George 200
RENAUDOT, Abbe 49 105
ROBB, Capt 171
ROBERTSON, Capt 121
ROGERS, 134 Maj 125 134 Robert 103
ROSE, Maj 81

INDEX

ROY, Rob 109
RUSH, Benjamin 158 Dr 98
SAINT, Clair 135 147 155 159 210 Clair Gen 148-152 Clair Gov 148
SARGENT, Col 148
SCHLOSSER, Ensign 128
SCOTT, Gen 154 Gov 174 Maj-gen 156-157
SCRIBNER, 221 Abner 220 Joel 220 Nathaniel 220
SHELBY, Gov 180 Isaac 138
SLAUGHTER, George 93
SLOUGH, Capt 150
SMILEY, Elder 99 Father 99-100
SMITH, 178 Mr 97-98 100
SNELLING, Capt 172
SPENCER, 170 Capt 171
STANWIX, John 193
STEUBEN, Baron 201
STEWART, John 138
TAYLOR, 63 233
TROTTER, Col 149
TRUEMAN, Maj 153
VANMETRE, 76
VIGO, Francis 234
VONKRELING, August 216
VONMULLER, Herr 216
WALKER, 233
WALLACE, David 77
WARWICK, Capt 171
WASHINGTON, 54-59 67 95 112 147 152-153 193 204 235 Augustus 231 Col 194 Gen 160 191 Lawrence 231-232 Mr 232
WAYNE, 155-156 174 Anthony 59 152 158 Gen 153-154 159-160 Mad Anthony 136 158
WEISER, 54
WEST, Benjamin 59
WETZEL, 89 97 Jacob 88 John 88 Lewis 88 90
WHITE, Isaac 171
WILLIAMSON, Col 78 David 77
WINANS, Mr 166
WINCHESTER, 175 Gen 174
WOLFE, 103
WOOD, Col 181
WYLLYS, Maj 148-149
ZANE, Elizabeth 63